the
wild & free
garden

TRANSFORM YOUR OUTDOOR SPACE
with Found Materials, Community
Sharing, and Creative Ingenuity

STEPHANIE ROSE
of Garden Therapy, author of *Garden Alchemy*
and *The Regenerative Garden*

COOL
SPRINGS
PRESS

Quarto.com

© 2026 Quarto Publishing
Text and Photos © 2026 Stephanie Rose

First Published in 2026 by Cool Springs Press, an imprint of The Quarto Group,
100 Cummings Center, Suite 265-D, Beverly, MA 01915, USA.
T (978) 282-9590 F (978) 283-2742

EEA Representation, WTS Tax d.o.o.,
Žanova ulica 3, 4000 Kranj, Slovenia.
www.wts-tax.si

Cool Springs Press titles are also available at discount for retail, wholesale, promotional, and bulk purchase. For details, contact the Special Sales Manager by email at specialsales@quarto.com or by mail at The Quarto Group, Attn: Special Sales Manager, 100 Cummings Center, Suite 265-D, Beverly, MA 01915, USA.

30 29 28 27 26   1 2 3 4 5

ISBN: 978-1-57715-639-0

Digital edition published in 2026
eISBN: 978-1-57715-640-6

Library of Congress Cataloging-in-Publication Data is available.

Design and Page Layout: Cindy Samargia Laun
Cover Images: Stephanie Rose
Photography: Stephanie Rose, except:
  Sue Goetz: Page 19
  Eduardo Cristo: Pages 23 and 113 (right)
  Austin Dennys: Page 44
  Susan Goble: Page 94
  Shutterstock: Pages 109 and 125
Illustration: Shutterstock

Printed in Guangdong, China TT112025

To those who
protect the trees,
save the bees,
and love with ease,
your seeds of kindness
grow the garden
of tomorrow.

contents

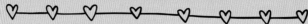

introduction

Sitting among the abundance of flowers, birds, and bees that grace the garden of my current home, it's hard to believe I was once homeless. To look around my garden, you would never be able to tell that this space was built from salvaged materials, clearance plants, and sheer determination. But that is the story of how I got here. You see, I've always been scrappy. Not scrappy in a "let's settle this in the parking lot" way, but in a "dandelion growing in the sidewalk" way; a natural resourcefulness that helped me through some tough times when I was younger has become the foundation of who I am.

In my teenage years, I was living on my own, attending high school and working at a shoe store making $4.12 an hour. I had to use creativity to manage my personal business while still being viewed legally as a child. It wasn't easy. A few times over those years, I lost my housing. Floating around with a modest garbage bag of possessions, I would spend a few nights in any place I could find, like a friend's car or in a small apartment with eleven other people. I traveled light and learned to be frugal with my spending to make ends meet. I accepted the generosity of friends' parents who would give me a place to stay or a bag of groceries. Those gestures taught me to never underestimate the power of kindness.

Years later my friends and colleagues were buying clothes and cars and condos, but after a long time of not having a secure home, I wanted a house. I found a blue bungalow in an emerging neighborhood that nobody wanted. It had been on the market for six months despite how hot the real estate market was. The owners had watched too many HGTV house-flip TV shows and lacked the basics in construction and home design. That didn't deter me. All I saw was the two-bedroom mortgage helper that would allow me to own a home for the same monthly price as my peers' rental apartments.

The blue bungalow's mortgage was at the top of my budget, so I made plans to fix it up using found materials, elbow grease, and a healthy dose of creativity. There were still some of the charming decorative features from its original construction in the 1930s, so I set out to restore the original hardwood floors, glass doorknobs, and fancy heat vent covers. Many years were spent searching classified ads, thrift shops, and salvage yards for secondhand materials that would bring a new life to the inside of the house.

Over those transformative years, I redesigned the gardens as well. The main structure was the back patio that I made from a used set of pavers found on Craigslist. The seller was only a fifteen-minute drive away, but that distance seemed much closer before I had to drive back with my Honda CR-V bottoming out from the weight. I mapped the patio layout on paper first to fit the design to the materials: a mix of small and large rectangular slabs. When the final stone fit in perfectly, it sparked both disbelief and celebration.

I filled the surrounding garden beds with perennials from friends' gardens and a few clearance-aisle trees. Resting in an old hammock under the deck was one of my favorite ways to enjoy the space, as was entertaining friends at the patio table I found in a back alley and refurbished. It was perfect: a unique, one-of-a-kind, bespoke outdoor living space that took five years and hundreds of memories to build. During my years in the blue bungalow, my revitalization efforts transformed a simple house into a home, and the garden into a space that welcomed family, friends, neighbors, and wildlife alike.

WHY QUALITY MATTERS

My time in the blue bungalow was more than twenty years and two houses ago. It seems like a lifetime has passed, given how much things have changed. Back then, it would have been much easier to purchase new materials from a big-box store than to hunt for reclaimed treasures, but I had more gumption than money. With a nonexistent budget, my biggest challenge was that I didn't want my home and garden to look "junky." My aesthetic is natural and artistic, not flea market finds. I sought high-quality materials that had endured well through their first use, proving they would perform far better than new cheaply manufactured materials designed for obsolescence.

In our current culture of overconsumption, we gravitate toward the conveniences of availability, low prices, and instant home delivery rather than the hunt-and-gather approach to collecting goods. Quality matters less than ever. Replacements are readily available and we rarely invest in heirlooms. It's increasingly disheartening to witness our elder generations unable to rehome their gold-rimmed wedding dishware or perfectly preserved birdseye maple headboards. Instead, people buy a $19.99 Costco dish set or $199 upholstered headboard, all of which will be broken and destined for the landfill in five years.

This mindset is also happening in our gardens. Mass-produced plastic planters have replaced stone urns or handcrafted ironwork that withstand decades of weather. Garden tools have become disposable, with flimsy handles and blades that bend after a season's use. The plants we choose are an expensive means of decorating a garden, rather than the treasured divisions from family and neighbors or prized heirlooms adopted at a botanical garden's gift shop.

I remain hopeful that this trend for cheap and cheerful is fading as quickly as the products get tossed in a dumpster. There is evidence this is the case. I see a renewed interest in heirlooms in our homes and gardens because the younger generations are turning to beauty, quality, and outstanding value. The choice to buy something that is better quality and more beautiful for the same price as a cheaply made new product is a logical decision, of course. The question remains, is it worth the time and effort?

There's truth in what our grandparents used to say:
"They don't make things like they used to!" Most of us
have probably muttered those same words ourselves.

THE HIGH COST OF INSTANT GARDENS

In 2020, the global pandemic forced people into isolation, but it also brought many of them closer to home, both physically and emotionally. Visits to my website, *Garden Therapy*, quadrupled as people searched for ways to connect with nature. While this surge in interest was inspiring, I couldn't help but worry that many new gardeners wouldn't stick with it. The way we've come to build (quick, costly, and unsustainable) gardens often sets people up for frustration rather than long-term success.

I watched that unfold through the front window of my second home. Not long after lockdowns began, a team of contractors arrived to build cedar raised beds on the sloped front yard of the brand-new half-duplex across the street. With shiny new lumber, shiny new soil, and shiny new vegetable seedlings, that instant garden was Instagram worthy. The installation and planting were finished in just two days, after which I became witness to the neighbors' extensive labor to manage these beds. The daily watering and weeding routine over the next five months produced a bounty of kale, beets, carrots, and tomatoes all ripening at the same time in midsummer. The cost for that garden was at least $5,000 to produce maybe $100 worth of homegrown veggies.

I'm not saying that there weren't many nonmonetary benefits like the pleasure of gardening and the beautification of the neighborhood. One might argue that the landscaping could have improved their home's resale value. The costs, however, made the project unsustainable. The labor required to manage that vegetable garden was unwavering. The location of the beds was in full sun, but not ideal for a vegetable garden because it was far from the home and not easy to access the beds. If they missed one day of watering in the summer, the harvest would fail. The materials that were used to build the instant garden could have been reclaimed, reducing the start-up costs. And the labor could have been done, at least in part, by the homeowners to instill pride in the space and respect for the effort it took to build, rather than the instant gratification of a social media–inspired makeover.

Sadly, my prediction was correct. The neighbor's garden was too labor-intensive for the benefits, and within two years the garden was overgrown and neglected. The homeowners eventually moved to Toronto and rented the duplex to another family. The new tenants haven't shown any interest in the garden project either. Today, the front-yard beds have become a graveyard for the pandemic-born enthusiasm for gardening that I had so dearly hoped would thrive.

This story is not isolated. I often listen to the enthusiastic tales of a brand-new garden "system" someone wants to install, like an exact replica of the trendy metal stock tank beds with an archway to grow pumpkins that had millions of views on an influencer's feed. A feed shows just a snippet of success, not the full story. The true cost isn't just the materials, it's the labor for building and maintenance; the materials needed to fill the beds; the energy needed to grow the food; and the waste that is created by using new materials when there is a mountain of usable second-hand materials on the way to the landfill.

When I watched my neighbor's garden being built, I wished I had this book to share with them to help them find practical solutions for a more sustainable project. I wanted to point them in the direction of reclaimed materials for the beds, saving on their initial investment and keeping new products out of the waste cycle. I longed to discuss soil-building techniques like sheet mulching and composting to promote healthier soil and plants. I wished I had mentioned how planting a polyculture of heirloom varieties and drought-tolerant pollinator plants alongside food crops could stagger the harvest, reduce water reliance, and naturally deter pests.

Even more, I wanted them to slow down and appreciate the process of building the garden. If they had built it over the summer, there would have been successes and great mistakes in the design that would have increased their knowledge and skills; careful choices made with the plants resulting in an investment in their health; perhaps some garden art or a found material made into a focal point that made them smile each time they watered or weeded. All of these would have been woven into a storybook of how the garden came to be; memories shared at dinner parties over homegrown vegetables that turned each meal into an offering of love, as well as nourishment.

My hope is that through the pages of this book, I can help you avoid fruitless efforts and discover materials and designs that let gardening take deep root in your soul. You won't find viral hacks or one-click solutions here, but you will find ideas that free you from the hustle, helping you spend less money, time, and effort while growing a more meaningful garden.

By returning to the practice of hunting and gathering, you'll engage in the process of making, revising, and expanding your creativity. You'll exercise your mind and rediscover the joy of slow, intentional work. You'll cultivate a greater appreciation for value, individuality, and history. You'll step off the hamster wheel of consumerism, freeing yourself from a cycle that drains both our well-being and the health of our planet. In slowing down, you'll rebalance your hormones, embracing the slow-release of dopamine that comes with delayed gratification. Most importantly, you'll feel the deep gratitude of the connections we build with our land and neighbors.

My wild & free vegetable garden was designed with items found in my neighborhood Buy Nothing group, gifted, or found in my shed. The bean arch and bistro set were online finds while the collection of planters and plant supports I've had for more than 10 years. I made the Free Range escargot sign in 2013 for my first book, *Garden Made*. Total cost: $0.

1

EMBRACING THE WILD AND FREE GARDENING MINDSET: ACCESSING ABUNDANCE

Collectively, we have enough stuff. In fact, we have too much. We have spurred whole offshoot businesses that recycle waste and resell unused goods. They help us declutter and regain control over our hearts and minds when the basement and garage are overflowing and we're being consumed by the things we own.

In the age of one-click buying and same-day shipping, we have easier access to just about anything we could possibly imagine; much that exceeds our wildest dreams. It stands to reason that people are acquiring more than they could ever possibly want or need, and that companies are producing more stuff, cheaper stuff, trendier stuff every minute that triggers signals in our brains to *buy now* and finally have the home/garden/life of our dreams.

How many clothes hang in the closet with tags still attached? What about the home or garden décor that never found a place to settle? Or the plants and bulbs that withered before we found space for them in the garden? The abundance of stuff has opened up every possibility, yet become our burden.

A few times a year, we roll up our sleeves and dive into decluttering and spring cleaning. We give our discards away, list them for sale, or decide how to recycle them. We feel especially attached to *brand-new in box* or *new without tags* items because they never fulfilled their destiny to beautify our lives or add value in some way. Instead, we finally release them back into the world for the next person.

I encourage you to pause for a moment and consider how many things you own but rarely use. Then multiply that by the people in your neighborhood, city, or country. If all those items were sold, donated, or posted in gift groups, we could easily create a secondhand marketplace that eliminated the need for much of what we currently buy new. Billions of products exist in closets and sheds, an inventory rivaling the largest online retailers. The more people who participate in the sharing economy, the more everyone benefits through savings, income, reduced waste, and newfound connections. This is where the Wild & Free Gardening mindset begins. We extract ourselves from the instant gratification circuit that leaves us empty amid clutter and reprogram our thinking. We learn to balance effort against consumption. We become

wild & free.

Easy-care groundcovers, shell mulch from a nearby beach, and found stones make this garden an elegant showcase without the need to purchase anything.

Wildness

This chapter is about trading orthodoxies for curiosity. We're going to forget the rules and throw out the to-do lists. I'm not going to describe what the perfect garden looks like and give you the DIY step-by-step instructions to make it happen. Instead, allow me to take your hand and guide you to discover your own wildness: your natural connection to the Earth, your garden, your creativity, your personal style, and the peace and joy that comes from individuality.

We'll explore through observation exercises that help you understand how you currently engage with your garden and natural spaces. You'll look at your individual garden's makeup: its function, how you use it, and its practical realities, like proximity to water, light patterns, existing energy, and structures. Assessing your garden's unique features allows for a starting point for you to design the garden of your dreams no matter where in the world you live: no matter your country, climate, landscape, or dwelling. Whether you have houseplants and a few herbs on the windowsill, a plot at the community garden, an urban city house with a small garden, a large suburban yard, a woodland retreat, or a hobby farm, this is where you come into your wildness.

Start with Wonder: An Invitation to Rediscover Nature

Your journey toward growing wild and free begins with an invitation to rediscover the nature that surrounds you. Gather a journal, some pens or pencils, and a nourishing beverage. Then head outside to the garden. Leave your phone inside and, while you're at it, pack away perfection, to-do lists, and worries as well.

Imagine you're a guest visiting the space for the first time.

Walk slowly and intentionally.

Breathe in the scents and listen to the sounds.

Use all your senses to bring yourself into presence and observe.

Jot down notes as you go, or simply embrace the feelings that arise.

When you're ready, find a comfortable place to sit and write in your journal. List everything you felt and thought in the garden: Every idea or observation, from tiny to tremendous, has a place on the page. Whether it flows as an orderly list or a tapestry of words and pictures, let whatever comes to you transfer onto the page. Draw the plants or pick flowers and press them between the pages. Add color and doodles. Bring your thoughts to life.

This is how we come into our wildness. From this place of openness, we see the garden with fresh eyes and renewed wonder.

Sue Goetz, a Tacoma, Washington-based horticulturist, herbalist, and garden designer, teaches garden journaling classes to bring together a deep love for art and plants.

create a wild & free garden journal

My mother's garden journal, which I discovered after she passed away, was a modest spiral-bound school notebook. As I thumbed through the pages, I saw her garden come together with interesting magazine and newspaper clippings pasted alongside her notes. It was beautiful; a keepsake of her garden that was well-organized and deeply personal, yet it didn't cost a penny to create.

Create your own garden journal with a found notebook and some decorative pressed flowers or images to make it your own. The act of creating a garden journal allows us to create a place for planning. The act of personalizing it, just as my mother did with her pasted articles, fosters value and attachment to the planning process and the record-keeping. Dedicate as much time to the project as you like, but the more personal it is, the more you will treasure it for years to come.

Tip

Add the date at the top of each new page you write and leave room for notes in the following years on those same pages. This way you can see how your garden grows not just over the season, but over the years.

MATERIALS:

- Notebook or journal (found, recycled, or repurposed)
- Pressed flowers, photographs, or paper images
- Decoupage adhesive or craft glue, like Mod Podge
- Paintbrush
- Clear contact paper, spray sealant, or access to lamination (optional)

1. You probably have a notebook in your home or office that could serve as a garden journal. Often we have books where we've jotted down a few notes or started a journal but never completed it; simply removing those pages can give us a fresh start. Or perhaps you have been given a promotional notebook from a business or event. If you don't have something that can be repurposed, many other people do, so look for them at Little Free Libraries, paper and book recycling depots, secondhand stores, and free groups.

2. Once you have your notebook, take some time to personalize it. Decoupaging the cover with pressed flowers brings us into our creativity and attaches a value to the notebook that no money could buy. This decoupage project could also be done with printed photos, images from seed catalogs, or old gardening books. The instructions are the same whether you use flowers or paper.

3. Arrange pressed flowers or other decorative elements on a sheet of paper to map out the final design. When you're happy with the arrangement, add another sheet of paper overtop and flip the flowers so they are upside down. This will help to preserve the layers of the design while you apply the underside to the cover first.

4. Allow to dry, then apply two to three thin layers of the adhesive over your decorated cover, allowing each layer to dry completely before applying the next.

5. Create sections for different garden areas or seasons, or just begin filling the pages with notes. It will come together as you work through your garden. Add plant lists, interesting articles, seed packets, and growing tips with lots of room for notes, sketches, and pressed plants.

THE NEUROSCIENCE BEHIND GARDEN JOURNALING

Have you noticed when you first discover something, you suddenly see it everywhere? Like when you spot a new-to-you plant at the garden center and the next day you realize it's growing in all your neighbors' gardens. That's your reticular activating system (RAS) at work, the network of neurons in our brainstem that acts as a gatekeeper for your awareness. It helps us notice what matters based on our beliefs, thoughts, and experiences.

You can train your RAS through activities like journaling. When you write down your goals, intentions, and garden design ideas, you're giving your brain clear instructions on what to prioritize. Journaling strengthens this effect by filling your RAS with information about what deserves attention.

When we combine this with gardening, there's an additional benefit from the therapeutic act itself. Gardening helps us focus on the present and notice signs of growth and progress. We pay attention to what's resilient and renewing, which rewires our thought patterns to help us see what's becoming rather than what's missing. Garden journaling doesn't just help us find what we're looking for; it also helps reset our intentions and reconnect us with nature.

Steps to Assess Your Garden Space

Assessing your garden space creates the roots for which wild and free designs will grow from. This is an exercise in both observation and note-taking. Get your garden journal and some colorful pencils ready to record your garden basics (like soil, light, and water), draw a garden map for each season, and make a wish list for the future of your space.

SOIL

I have lived in four different homes all within a kilometer of each other and each has such wildly different soil. In my first house, the soil was pale brown, dry, dusty, and devoid of any life. In my second home, the soil was filled with buried construction materials and sand from a past renovation. In my third, a brand-new build, the soil was deeply compacted from the house construction and lacked organic materials. In my current home, the soil is black, loamy, and full of worms, but the water table is so high that the garden floods in the winter and spring. In all cases, removing the debris, then nourishing the soil with organic matter, improved the soil structure, nutrients, and overall health.

To assess your garden soil, dig a few holes in the garden with your trowel and observe the soil. Feel it with your hands, smell it, and look closely, even using a magnifying glass to see more detail. Look at the plants in it and any signs of pests or disease.

Next, write down words that describe your soil's health. Some examples:

Healthy soil:
- Dark or rich color
- Loose and free draining
- Moist or holds moisture
- Rich in organic matter
- Visible soil organisms (like worms, beetles, millipedes, and fungus)
- Robust, healthy plants growing

Unhealthy soil:
- Dusty
- Compacted
- Saturated
- Full of debris (like construction materials, concrete, rocks, and trash)
- Visible disease or pest issues
- Sickly plants

IT STARTS WITH THE SOIL

At this stage, we are only observing the soil as an assessment. I have written much more about improving soil in my book on permaculture for the home garden: *The Regenerative Garden*. If you don't have a copy, here is a key takeaway: No matter what issues you have with your soil, the structure improves by adding organic matter. Top the garden beds with well-rotted compost twice a year and it will take care of most soil concerns.

LIGHT

Light conditions can vary greatly across your garden and throughout the seasons. In this section, make general notes about the gardens' usual light (such as full sun, part sun, part shade, shade) and how it changes by season.

- **Full Sun:** A minimum of 6 hours of sun in the hottest part of the day (generally between 10 a.m. to 4 p.m.). Plants labeled as "full sun" perform better when they are in direct sunlight, even in the heat of the day.

- **Part Sun:** From 4 to 6 hours of direct sun, including the warm afternoon sun. Plants labeled as "part sun" require at least some direct sunlight to thrive.

- **Part Shade:** From 4 to 6 hours of direct sun in the morning or evening, when it's cooler. Plants labeled as "part shade" require at least some shade as relief from the hottest part of the day, as full sun would be too intense.

- **Shade:** From 2 to 4 hours of direct sun, but not zero. Plants labeled as "shade" still need sunlight, preferably in the morning, but can survive with minimal sun.

- **Deep Shade:** From 0 to 2 hours of direct sun. Most plants need some sunlight to grow, so there is a very limited number of plants that can thrive in deep shade.

This garden is planted on the East side of the property beside a shed. The front part of the garden gets hot afternoon sun so it is planted with drought tolerant native sedums. The back part of the garden gets mostly shade so it is planted with shade-tolerant ferns and epimedium.

WATER

To understand your garden's water story, start by mapping where water lives and moves on your property. Walk around and locate your outdoor taps, existing irrigation systems, rain barrels, and any natural spots where water tends to collect. If you know which direction water flows from your land and where the water table runs high or low, jot that down too, as this knowledge becomes incredibly valuable when planning what to plant where.

Spend time observing how water behaves in your space, especially during and after rain. Notice the low spots where puddles form and the slopes where water rushes past. Watch for runoff patterns and see how your roof, driveway, or patio might be directing water in unexpected ways. Some areas will stay boggy or flood seasonally, while others turn bone dry by midsummer despite your best efforts. These aren't problems to solve immediately; they're clues about what your land wants to do naturally.

Sketch a simple map showing how water moves through your property. Mark your sources, storage areas, and the spots that stay wet or dry. This becomes your water roadmap for future planting and improvement decisions.

A rain chain helps to redirect water from the roof to garden pots or a rain barrel.

PLANTS

Your plants tell the story of what thrives in your specific conditions. Start by listing the main characters: the larger trees and shrubs that create your garden's structure and personality. These foundational plants shape everything else in your space, from the light patterns they create to the shelter they provide.

Work your way down through the layers: shrubs that fill the middle story, perennials that return year after year, any lawn areas, and bulbs that pop up seasonally. Don't forget to include both ornamental and edible plants. Note where each plant or group of plants lives, what conditions they prefer, positive observations (for example, fragrant in winter, blooms without fail, striking fall color,

and so on), and any ongoing struggles you have noticed (like pests or disease, yellowing leaves, not blooming, and so on).

Pay attention to any pest or disease issues you've noticed, but at this stage, simply assess and note your observations. Stay on track with the assessment and make a note to come back to problem solve at a later time.

As you continue to research and build your garden assessment, dig a little deeper. Look up the botanical name if you don't know it, and record details like mature size, when it flowers or fruits, and growing conditions.

Trees: Japanese maple 'Bloodgood' (*Acer palmatum atropurpureum* 'Bloodgood') Grows to 15–20 feet (4.6–6.1 m) tall and wide; can tolerate full sun to part shade as long as the soil is moist and well-drained. Always thrives in spring and fall, but in summer needs constant watering to keep leaf tips from burning. Burgundy leaves have five or seven points and turn brilliant red in fall. Note: Move to a shadier location in winter when dormant.

Shrubs: Fire Light panicle hydrangea (*Hydrangea paniculata* 'Fire Light') Grows 6–8 feet (1.8–2.4 m) tall and wide; prefers full sun to part shade, but dislikes overly moist or soggy soil. Produces large cone-shaped blooms that can become heavy and flop, especially after rain. Prune back by one-third in early spring to manage size and shape. Frequently admired by passersby; some stems have been broken off by people taking cuttings.

Perennials: Purple coneflower (*Echinacea purpurea*) – Grows to nearly 4 feet (1.2 m) tall; loves full sun; drought tolerant once established. This native variety performs better than the hybrid varieties, holds well as cut flowers, and is loved by bees. Medicinal properties are beneficial for immune function. Make a tincture from dried root, flowers, and leaves in the fall.

Bulbs: Tête-à-Tête Narcissus (*Narcissus* 'Tête-à-Tête') – Grows 6–8 inches (15–20 cm) tall; thrives in full sun to part shade with well-drained soil. Planted in lawn alongside grape hyacinth (*Muscari armeniacum*) for a striking midspring display. Leaves remain messy after flowering until surrounding wildflowers fill in and provide cover.

MICROCLIMATES

Your garden contains smaller zones that behave differently based on sun, wind, shelter, and elevation, and garden needs can vary greatly in these microclimates. Walk your space at various times throughout the day and across seasons to determine what these microclimates are. Does it feel warmer by the stone wall in spring? Does the pond at the front of the garden freeze first? Observe unique events and you'll discover microclimates. On cool days, look for corners that stay surprisingly warm on cold mornings, spots where frost clings long after it's melted everywhere else, and areas where snow disappears first. Pay attention to heat that bounces off your house, driveway, or south-facing fence that can create warm conditions just a few feet from cooler zones. Look for sheltered nooks where tender plants might survive winter, and identify exposed areas where even hardy plants struggle against harsh conditions.

WIND

Walk around and notice how air moves through your space. Does wind funnel between your house and the neighbor's garage, creating a wind tunnel effect? Are there spots completely sheltered by mature trees or structures? Your plants will show you the evidence, such as leaning stems that permanently bend away from prevailing winds; leaves with brown, crispy edges from constant drying; or broken branches that couldn't withstand the pressure. Make note of seasonal patterns and determine if you need to install windbreaks.

SLOPE AND TOPOGRAPHY

Even the flattest-looking yard has subtle changes in elevation that dramatically affect how water behaves and where plants will thrive. Slopes should drain water away from buildings, and perhaps into ponds, rain gardens, or storm drains. After a good rain, take a walk and watch where water goes. You'll spot the low areas where puddles linger for days and the higher ground that sheds water quickly. Notice any erosion patterns: those little channels where water has carved its preferred path. Some slopes are so gradual, you barely notice them until you see how they direct water flow. Make notes of any plants and hardscape materials (like rocks, concrete, and wood) installed to level and hold elevation changes.

WILDLIFE AND INSECTS

Look for the telltale signs of who's visiting when you're not around: rabbit droppings under your favorite shrubs, perfectly round holes in hosta leaves (courtesy of slugs), or deer browse lines where everything gets nibbled to the same height. Don't just focus on the troublemakers. Watch for the good guys too.

WONDERFUL WINDBREAKS

A well-placed tree or fence can shield an area up to five times its height. For example, a 5-foot (1.5 m) fence provides wind protection for 25 feet (8 m) beyond it.

Opposite above left: This rooftop garden acts as a hardworking greenspace to beautify the yard to create a sound dampening barrier from the trains. Opposite above right: Fences and plants create privacy and wind protection. Opposite below left: A concrete block wall retains the upper level garden and has pockets for planting. Opposite below right: Notice which flowers attract the most bees, where birds like to perch, and whether you've got beneficial insects like ladybugs and hoverflies.

HUMAN USE AND MOVEMENT

Watch where people naturally walk, even if there's no official path. Notice the spots where kids like to play or where you find yourself lingering with your morning coffee. Pay attention to areas that get heavy foot traffic and end up compacted, and identify those forgotten corners that nobody ever visits. These observations reveal where hardscape makes sense, where you need tough, treadable plants, and where you can place more delicate specimens.

This path wasn't in the original garden design, but was added after the neighborhood teens forged a shortcut to the front door from the sidewalk.

How to Create a Garden Map, and Why It's Important

Creating a garden map isn't about documenting one perfect moment in time. Instead, it's about creating a living record that grows and changes just as your space does. The best practice would be to watch your garden through a whole year and noting the seasonal shifts, especially if you're still getting to know the property. Even if you've been there for years, committing to a year of really paying attention will surprise you with what you discover.

This doesn't mean putting your shovel away for 12 months. Keep gardening over the time and building on your assessment; you can always make changes as you learn more. The documenting becomes part of the story, helping you figure out why some areas thrive while others seem to struggle. In doing this exercise, you might finally understand water, soil, and plant issues or successes that you didn't anticipate. It's this long-term observation that makes you a better partner to your land.

Start by accessing a satellite image of your property through Google Earth or a property map from local records. Print the image, place tracing paper over it, and outline your property boundaries. You can use city dimensions for precise measurements if needed.

Mark all existing elements:
- Paths and walkways
- Structures (like the house, shed, and outbuildings)
- Water sources
- Trees and established plants
- Garden beds

In your garden journal, write a comprehensive key to the map along with a plant list that includes botanical names. Online resources can help with identification of the plants you don't know. Remember, this list doesn't have to be done in one afternoon. You can add to your list as you become more familiar with plants that share your space.

GARDEN WISH LIST

Once you have your map created, you can make a few more copies to start playing with design ideas. Make a list of the structures and foundation plantings you want to add or change. It can be general, such as, "I want a tree here for shade to protect us from the sun when we're sitting on the patio," "I want patio pavers in this area," "I want a new shed," or "I want to plant a pollinator garden." Or it can be more specific, with detailed plants and structures that add to your space. You can have multiple designs with differing themes as wish lists and add to them as you develop more needs or wants. A wish list is meant to allow you the freedom to dream.

With the wish list in mind, you will have a guide for what you want to add or take away from your garden when you are involved in your sharing communities. For instance, you might have an arbor on your wish list when someone in your Buy Nothing group is giving away scrap lumber. Or you might see a tree on a lot slated for demolition. With wish lists prepared, you can jump on these opportunities quickly, which is often needed when great stuff is offered up for free.

SEASONAL MAPPING

Seasonal mapping reveals crucial information about environmental factors that a single observation would miss. For instance, your full-sun garden might become part shade in summer when the large deciduous street trees leaf out. In winter, buildings can cast longer shadows as the sun sits lower in the sky, making some parts of the garden damp and muddy. Or tender plants might come back unexpectedly the next year in some parts of the garden, simply because of the warmer microclimate created by the structures surrounding the area.

Once you have your base map, photocopy it a number of times to record seasonal changes. Start with four copies for each of the four seasons: spring, summer, autumn, and winter. Then map the sun path, shadow patterns, and light classifications.

Sun Path

Record the sun path by noting morning sunrise time, position, and direction with arrows on your map. Mark the noon sun position when it reaches its highest point in the sky. Record evening sunset time, position, and direction using arrows to show how the sun moves across your property throughout the day.

Shadow Pattern

Record shadow patterns by drawing areas shaded by tree canopies directly on your map. Include shadows cast by structures such as your house, shed, and fences to see how they affect growing conditions.

Light Classification

Create light classifications by marking areas that receive full sun, part sun, part shade, full shade, and deep shade. Add specific notes about any unusual light conditions or seasonal variations that might affect plant growth.

Using Permaculture Zones to Design Your Space

Permaculture zones are a way of organizing the plants in your yard depending on accessibility and energy. They are meant to help you in the designing and planning part of your garden to help conserve energy and maintenance. With zones, you're left with effective, efficient, and ethical gardens.

Zones aren't meant to be rigid and circular. They're flexible, invisible lines with no boundaries. They're meant to blend together and can be any shape or size. No one's permaculture zones will look alike. No matter what your garden space is, you can create zones based on using all your different spaces.

This can range from an apartment with no patio to a complete homestead. If you're growing plants and interested in permaculture, then you can apply these zones; albeit, some may expand beyond your property. For instance, a city house will have some zones on the property, but others will be in the community. In this case, the large fruit trees and perennials can fit in the backyard, but the Farm Zone might be a community supported agriculture (CSA) subscription and the Woodland Zone would be a local forest.

Read through the following zones and make notes in your garden journal as to how they relate to you and your garden space. Make notes about how often they are used, and the structure, function, plants, water sources, and energy. This will give you the guide for the best placement of your garden elements, and identify what is needed.

Using zones as a planning tool will ensure you don't plant a shrub too far away from a water source for you to easily access, that your herbs are readily snippable while cooking, and that your morning walk to collect the chicken eggs doesn't involve a hike to the other side of your property.

ZONE 0: HOME

Your home is your immediate zone, the place that you use daily, covering every inch of your living space. The function is to support the self. It's where we find safety, rest, and nourishment. We decorate with art and surround the space with things we love, while performing our daily routines to wash, prepare food, work, entertain, and relax. The plants inside this zone could be houseplants, indoor herbs, sprouts, microgreens, seedlings, and harvests that are being processed for preservation.

With a large movement of people gardening inside the home, it's becoming increasingly important to map out the Home Zone. If houseplants are just one of the types of gardening you do, this is where you will include them. On the other hand, if you only have indoor plants and they are the primary gardening that you do, then read through all of the zones and see where some of your houseplant babies are managed. For instance, the Home Zone might be the kitchen, where you grow herbs on the windowsill and bring all the plants in for repotting, while the living room, bathrooms, bedroom, basement, and storage space could be different zones.

The Home Zone also includes the practices you're doing in your home to better the environment and local ecosystem. This can mean everything from shorter showers to growing seedlings to donate to a community project.

What we're aiming for in this zone is pretty straightforward: Conserve energy where we can, grow small amounts of food (even if it's just herbs on a windowsill), make and store what we eat, reduce waste, and use materials from nearby when possible. Think: herbs growing in your kitchen, a little compost collection spot under your sink, maybe a worm farm if you're feeling adventurous, or jars of sprouts growing on your counter. Even your pets are part of this system because they affect how you use your space and resources.

Top: Thinking about your home this way helps you see all the small changes that can give you that connection with nature, even when indoors. Bottom: Even your pets are part of this system because they affect how you use your space and resources.

ZONE 1: GARDEN

Right outside your home is where the garden zone begins. This is your most intensively cared-for outdoor space, the area you'll visit daily, so it needs to be easily accessible. We're talking about everything immediately surrounding your home: front yard, backyard, porch, balcony, or deck space.

This is where you might start seeing garden structures appear: patio for morning coffee, compost bin, rain barrel, bird feeder, or vegetable beds. These aren't just random additions; they're all working together to create a more efficient, productive space. Again, how you determine the zone is by use, not the definition of garden. In a large homestead, you might also have a small pond, cold frames, or a potting shed in the Garden Zone. Additionally, you can have multiple Zone 1s: Unique gardens located all close to the house with differing purposes, like the herb garden right outside the front door, the shade plants by the back patio, or the window boxes.

What you're working toward is managing energy expenditure by placing regularly accessed garden spaces in close proximity to the Home Zone; for instance, herbs and salad greens you like to eat daily, flowers that attract beneficial insects, berries that need to be picked as soon as they ripen, small shrubs that provide fragrance, and dwarf trees that add to the ambiance. By keeping our high-maintenance garden activities close to home, you can keep up on daily tasks, manage pest populations, and keep an eye on harvests, creating a space that feels harmonious rather than harrowing.

Top: Kale flowers are delicious in salads and as a garden snack. Center: Planting a variety of vegetables in succession means smaller, more consistent harvests over a longer season. Bottom: Cold frames made from re-purposed windows help to extend the growing season.

ZONE 2: FOOD FOREST

The food forest sits just beyond your intensive garden space and becomes mostly self-sustaining once established. The jobs are mainly pruning and harvesting rather than constantly tending. You'll still visit most days, but it requires way less daily attention than your vegetable beds.

This is where you might place larger structures that need space but not constant access: a greenhouse, bigger compost system, storage shed, small barn, beehives, or a little orchard. There may be months of the year that you need to work in these areas regularly, but not year-round. These elements work together to create a productive ecosystem that takes care of itself with less human input needed.

On a smaller lot, this could be the fruit and nut trees planted near the back of the property, the perennial vegetables and herbs that come back every season, or the city fruit trees that you can harvest and preserve. This space creates a habitat for wildlife and produces enough to share with neighbors and community.

ZONE 3: FARM

The farm is where you think bigger and longer-term. Maybe it's a larger orchard that produces enough fruit to sell at farmers' markets, grazing fields for farm animals, field shelters, or crops specifically grown to feed those animals. You're working with broader landscapes now, thinking about how water moves across the land and where you can store equipment and harvest.

For apartment dwellers and urban gardeners, the Farm Zone could be a community garden plot, a CSA membership, shared interest in a neighbor's garden, a cut-flower garden for a side business, or even houseplant propagation for trade or sale to support your growing indoor plant collection.

It's not the space that matters; it's in the intent of the production. The Farm Zone can be crops that you can use to reduce your overall costs, trade in your community, or sell to earn income. This zone is about scale and efficiency rather than daily tending. You're managing land, not just gardening, and the decisions you make here affect not just your household but potentially give you the opportunity to add to your economic well-being.

ZONE 4: WOODLAND

The Woodland Zone requires almost no care and stays mostly natural, like a trail through the forest that needs only annual brush clearing. This area sits beyond your farmland, often requiring a drive or longer hike to reach. Depending on where you live, it might look like dense forest, rivers, ponds, or meadows. This land is rich with native plants and wildlife and a source of materials, medicine, and wild food. On this land, you become a gatherer and steward rather than a gardener. You're harvesting what nature provides, like mushrooms, medicinal plants, berries, and timber for building projects.

Your role is more about careful taking than active growing. When you do intervene, it's with practices like reseeding and releasing spores to encourage new generations of growth, or controlled burns, selective tree harvesting, and planting native species. Urban gardeners may take to foraging in allowed public spaces, camping on the land, or taking part in educational forest tours.

In this zone, your relationship with the land is reciprocal. Your efforts are minimal, but you are also acting in the ecosystem's best interest, taking time to learn about the plants and animals, their names, their function, and their history. You take only what you need while ensuring there's more for the future. The woodland provides materials you can't grow in your garden zones, connects you to wild food traditions, and reminds you that some of the most valuable things require patience and respect.

ZONE 5: WILD FOREST

The final zone is wild forest: completely free from human maintenance or interference. You might visit weekly if you're an outdoor enthusiast or monthly if you just need to remember what truly wild looks like. These are old-growth forests, areas far from skyscrapers and towns. These lands need our protection to remain truly wild. That could mean staying away altogether, but it could also mean visiting with respect. When you visit, don't collect anything or change the landscape, but take the opportunity to learn from it.

Why does the forest matter for your overall design? Because healthy wild spaces stabilize soil and water systems that affect everything downstream, including your garden. They maintain wildlife populations that keep ecosystems balanced, prevent erosion that would otherwise affect waterways, and support rivers that provide clean water for communities. Most importantly, they remind us that not everything needs to be useful to humans to have value. Sometimes the most radical thing we can do is step back and let nature be nature, knowing that our restraint is actually the most productive choice we can make.

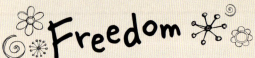 Freedom

The idea of breaking off from the rat race and living the life of your dreams: Sounds expensive, doesn't it? This is what we have been sold as a reward *after* hard work. That through suffering our jobs for the majority of our years, that we can get a taste of freedom in the form of a vacation or retirement. Which, of course, means we are not free at all.

What I mean by "freedom" is to step out from the cycle of consumerism that's become our default path and forge a new one. It's the movement toward "buy nothing" or "low buy," instead of ultimate convenience. When we spend less, we're not feeding the profits of massive organizations where a few multibillionaires hold all the wealth. Instead, we can work within our communities and share with each other.

Freedom means not just unchaining yourself from capitalism's confines, but from the assumption that you need to spend money to have a stylish, well-crafted garden. You don't. There are endless opportunities to find high-quality, beautiful pieces that express your individuality. Unlike mass-produced decor, these finds often carry character and history. You're curating art, not just filling space.

A spluttering frog fountain, a trio of classic urns, or a timeless black trellis for climbing plants will never go out of style. Each piece is unique, chosen by you, and becomes part of a home or garden that feels individual, not manufactured.

Whole communities are organizing to make this abundance more visible and accessible. Buy Nothing groups and secondhand marketplaces are popping up everywhere; businesses are redistributing goods to keep them out of the waste cycle; and communities and governments are supporting the efforts. The convenience and mass production of so much stuff has created a huge secondary problem with waste. It's no longer possible to turn a blind eye to the dumpsters full of brand-new goods and food waste, the mountains of fast fashion, or the swirling garbage islands in the ocean. In the second part of this chapter, we will look at how it's not just opportunistic to stop buying new and start finding free; it's a solution to the waste crisis. We will relearn the lost art of bartering and trade, how to find and access goods for free, and the skills to make use of government programs that can support these efforts. You aren't just saving money, you are helping to solve a much larger issue facing us all.

Beyond Money: Bartering and Trade

While bartering was once commonplace, it's not sustainable at the global scale of trade that we use today. The shift away from bartering meant losing the personalization and community building aspects that were woven into the transactions. Modern bartering is bringing back these connections within our communities.

Bartering is typically a trade of like—skills for skills, or goods for goods—but it can take many forms. The value is variable and negotiated in the initial stages of bartering. For goods-based bartering, people sometimes post in online marketplaces that they're looking to sell something but would "consider an exchange for" specific items they're seeking. If there's a match, a trade can happen determined by the agreed upon worth between the parties.

In a skills-for-skills barter, two parties trade a service in their expertise to help the other. This can be a single trade or ongoing relationship. As an example, a gardener could trade garden maintenance with a friend who does bookkeeping and taxes. They could trade the services once or create an ongoing relationship to trade their services with each other annually.

Goods-based bartering is often used in rural communities, where farmers trade farm products like eggs for honey or cabbages for potatoes on an ongoing basis. This serves to allow them to use their excess harvest to diversify their consumable products. There is an increasing trend toward this in younger generations, who will happily trade supplies, clothing, art, instruments, home goods, and of course garden supplies and plants.

Bartering could also be based on the relationship between ownership and labor surrounding an item. For instance, one gardener could lend their hedge-shearing tool to a neighbor on an ongoing basis and in return they would trim their shared hedge a few times a year. This approach works especially well in smaller, tighter communities where people know each other. Intentional communities like co-housing, co-ops, and connected neighborhoods are good examples. When individuals are more isolated from their neighbors or those living nearby, platform-based solutions like bartering apps can help these exchanges of goods or services.

There are countless ways in which bartering can occur, but the true beauty of bartering lies in the relationships it builds. When we trade directly, we create personal connections while avoiding the fees and complexity of conventional commerce. Though it can't replace our entire economic system, small-scale bartering adds richness to community life and reminds us of the value in direct exchange.

Geranium ('Johnson's Blue') is such a prolific perennial that it can always be divided and used for bartering with neighbors.

The Modern-Day Sharing Economy Explained

In 2020, people started working from home due to the COVID-19 pandemic. Our social behaviors shifted; not just in what we were mandated to do, like isolating and social distancing, but in how we collectively searched for community beyond the workplace. In particular, I noticed how many more people were spending time in front yards, building gardens, growing food, and beautifying their homes: not just gardening, but *gardening visibly*, where neighbors and friends could stop by to say hello or admire the work.

Without office water cooler conversations, people needed new ways to connect. Neighborhoods became the gathering places. People walked their blocks more, and front-yard gardening became more than just a hobby. It became a way to feel connected.

In my East Vancouver neighborhood, I saw an explosion of shared spaces. Little Free Libraries multiplied, joined by seed libraries, flower stands, plant swaps, and creative community offerings of every kind. Bins of toys for kids, shared dog libraries with treats and leashes, and little free art galleries were popping up everywhere. These spaces became part of daily life: ways to regift, reduce waste, and connect with neighbors. The sharing economy isn't just about saving money. It's about building stronger communities, reducing waste, and creating a better world.

Look around your neighborhood and you'll probably find examples of the sharing economy already happening. Here are some common ones:

Seed Swaps and Plant Swaps: Look for local gardening groups, libraries, nonprofits, or community centers that host Seedy Saturday events or plant swaps.

Community Compost Programs: Many municipalities or nonprofits offer free compost or mulch to residents, usually collected from local green waste programs.

Public Land Gardening Programs: Cities let residents "adopt" boulevards, curbside strips, or vacant lots for gardening. These programs often include permits and gardening support to get new gardeners started.

Tool Libraries: Find tool lending at community centers or through neighborhood groups that allow residents to borrow gardening equipment for little or no cost.

A little free seed library is a classic example of the sharing economy.

How to Navigate the Sharing Economy Online

Somewhere online right now, someone is offering exactly what you need for free. And tomorrow, you might be the one with something perfect for a neighbor you've never met. The Internet turned sharing from a neighborhood thing into a global gift exchange that never stops. Getting started is simpler than you think: no special memberships, no complicated sign-ups; just you, your computer, and communities of people who believe in abundance over scarcity. The coming pages share where to find them.

BUY NOTHING GROUPS

Buy Nothing and Freecycle groups are online organizations that offer community sharing. These groups run on the principle of giving: members offer items for free and others can ask for or claim what they need. It's a local circular economy of generosity that cuts waste and builds neighborhood connections.

When you're offering something, include photos, a quick description, and important details like condition, size, and pickup times. When you're asking for something, be specific and polite.

Popular items get lots of requests, so be patient. Check if the group requires in-person transfer to foster community connections or if porch pickups (leaving items outside) are preferred. Overall, make exchanges friendly, simple, and safe.

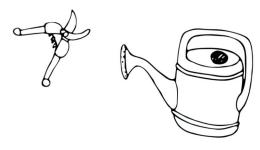

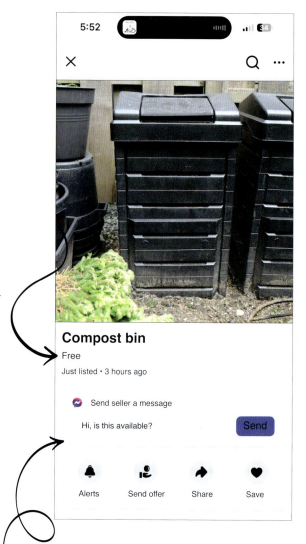

Compost bin

Free

Just listed • 3 hours ago

Send seller a message

Hi, is this available?   Send

Alerts   Send offer   Share   Save

FIND LOCAL ONLINE COMMUNITIES

Search Facebook for "Buy Nothing [Your Neighborhood]" or try your area plus "Freecycle." Check Freecycle.org and plug in your location to find nearby groups. Ask neighbors or look at community bulletin boards, libraries, local newsletters. Lots of Buy Nothing groups spread through word of mouth.

KEEP IT GREEN MATERIAL REUSE

While working in the film industry, Kelsey Evans was horrified at how many useable items were disposed of at the end of every project. Set materials would often end up in the landfill, when they could be reused. So Kelsey started Keep It Green Recycling Reuse in British Columbia, Canada in 2017 which now collects these materials from the film industry for a fee, and redistributes them to the community for free. There is plenty of garden goodies to be found like lumber, paper, planters, landscape fabric, and furniture.

Fresh cut flowers from the garden can be given as gifts in jars from the recycling bin.

BUY AND SELL CLASSIFIED ADS

Gone are the days when classified ads in the newspaper were the way to connect with the community. Now, classified ads are on Craigslist, Facebook Marketplace, and other buy and sell marketplaces online.

While these platforms generally are for buying and selling goods, they often have "free" sections where you can offer or search for free items. Many also have "in search of" (ISO) sections, so you can post requests for specific things you need. These platforms work differently than Buy Nothing groups because they're less about community building and more about quick exchanges, but are excellent at reaching a wider audience.

SEARCHING FOR FREE ITEMS ONLINE
- Use the filters to select "free" under pricing.
- Set up alerts or bookmark your searches so you get notified when new free items are posted.
- Check regularly, because free stuff items get exchanged quickly.
- Post your own ISO listings to let people know what you're hunting for.

GIVING AWAY FREE ITEMS ONLINE
- When you're giving stuff away, post clear photos and honest descriptions, especially if the item is broken, missing parts, or expired.
- Include pickup instructions and be ready for quick responses.
- Meet in public places for pickups, or arrange porch pickup when possible.
- Suggest people bring help for heavy items.

Opposite: This outdoor bath with propane shower, clear roof, and stained-glass windows is the kind of treasure you can find on an online marketplace. The owner, Austin Dennys, created this garden oasis from 80% recycled materials, including the stained glass windows he salvaged from a heritage building in downtown Victoria, British Columbia.

Scraps of materials can be shared and reused for new purposes, like this fencing used as plant supports.

NEIGHBORHOOD APPS AND NETWORKS

Many neighborhoods have email groups, social media groups, or apps that connect neighbors directly. For instance, Nextdoor is a neighborhood app where people give away items, lend tools, and post community events. These networks are often started by residents and run by volunteers. Community center pages and bulletin boards (digital or physical) usually include sharing opportunities too.

These neighborhood networks are goldmines for borrowing tools, finding supplies, organizing carpools, or getting recommendations for local services. Post what you need or what you're offering. People often share garden surplus or lend specialized equipment like pressure washers or ladders.

The key is being an active member, not just someone who asks for stuff. Share local news, offer help when you can, and celebrate your neighbors' wins. These groups work best when everyone contributes.

To find these groups, search "[your neighborhood] group" or ask at local coffee shops, libraries, or community centers. Many require you to verify your address before joining. Once you're in, introduce yourself and read the group guidelines as each community has its own vibe and rules.

Finding Your Gardening Community: Garden Clubs and Plant Groups

Join a garden group and you'll tap into a network of people who have more plants than space, more seeds than time, and more knowledge than you can imagine. Join one group and suddenly you have access to decades of collective wisdom and surplus resources. These communities are treasure troves of seeds, plants, tools, compost, expert advice, and connections. You just have to pick one.

COMMUNITY GARDENS

Community gardens are the most visible gardening groups and easy to join, although there may be a wait list. You will have instant access to a plot of land and perhaps shared access to compost, tools, and likely plant divisions and seedlings from other members. Community garden plots often require participating in shared work parties, which can be very social in addition to beneficial to the garden as a whole. There's always someone who knows why your tomatoes are splitting, has extra seedlings they started too many of, or can teach you crop rotation while you're both weeding.

GARDEN CLUBS AND HORTICULTURAL SOCIETIES

Garden clubs are nonprofit organizations, typically organized by city or town, that host structured meetings, have membership lists, and often have a long history in the community. Many host monthly speakers, plant swaps, flower shows, seed exchanges, and garden tours. Some offer

access to private gardens, discounts at nurseries, or even grants for local green projects. Joining one connects you to many experienced gardeners; some are backyard hobbyists, while others are professionals in the field. In my experience speaking to these groups around the world, they are consistently generous with their time and knowledge. You'll find mentors, trade partners, and sometimes lifelong friends.

MASTER GARDENER EXTENSIONS

Master Gardener programs are run through university extensions, botanical gardens, or local institutions. Their mission is to educate the public and support community-based gardening projects. Many chapters receive annual funding to help with local initiatives, offering free or low-cost resources like plant materials, soil testing, workshops, and expert guidance. These programs are a cornerstone of the gardening sharing economy. They make horticultural knowledge accessible, support school and community gardens, and reduce the cost of greening public spaces. Whether you're looking for help starting a pollinator garden or need advice on pruning fruit trees, there's likely a Master Gardener nearby who's happy to help.

PERMACULTURE AND ENVIRONMENTAL GROUPS

Permaculture and environmental groups focus on regenerative practices, ecological design, and sustainable living. They often bring people together through hands-on workshops, work parties, garden builds, and seasonal celebrations. These groups are deeply committed to the sharing economy. Free seeds, perennial plant divisions, tool lending, and group work days are common. Instead of encouraging consumption, they promote collaboration, resourcefulness, and mutual support. They may also offer a Permaculture Design Certificate (PDC) course, which provides in-depth training in sustainable land use, food systems, and community

design. Completing a PDC connects you to a global network of designers and growers working to create resilient ecosystems and communities.

INDIGENOUS GROUPS AND LAND CARE SOCIETIES

Indigenous land and food sovereignty organizations provide vital leadership in ecological stewardship and community-based resilience. Their work draws support from funding sources prioritizing traditional ecological knowledge, food security, and cultural continuity. If you're Indigenous, connecting with these organizations provides access to community-led projects, traditional knowledge, and cultural restoration funding. If you're not Indigenous, support this work by backing projects, sharing information widely, and offering help when invited.

Learning Spaces for Community-Minded Gardeners

Education spaces are where gardeners come together to learn and share what they know. These places offer more than facts; they create connection, spark new ideas, and encourage sharing. Whether it's a botanical garden, a university, or your local library, getting involved opens the door to a community that cares about growing plants and supporting each other.

BOTANICAL GARDENS

Botanical gardens serve as living libraries of plant knowledge. Visiting throughout the year lets you observe planting techniques, design elements, and seasonal changes you can apply in your own space. These gardens are designed to inspire, with features like art, seating areas, water systems, and wildlife habitat. Staff and volunteers are often generous with their knowledge, happy to answer questions or offer tips. Many botanical gardens also offer workshops, classes, and newsletters to help you keep learning and stay connected with the gardening community.

UNIVERSITIES AND COLLEGES

Local universities, especially those with environmental science, agriculture, or sustainability programs, often support community education through research and outreach. Faculty and students work on real-world projects that connect them with local gardeners, and many are eager to share what they're learning. These institutions may host garden tours, public lectures, volunteer projects, or seasonal events that showcase sustainable practices and experimental techniques. Getting involved offers access to up-to-date information, practical demonstrations, and a network of people exploring new ways to grow and live in harmony with nature.

COMMUNITY CENTERS AND LIBRARIES

Community centers and libraries are often the heart of local connection. They host gardening workshops, speaker series, seed libraries, and skill-sharing events that bring neighbors together. Libraries curate books and digital resources on everything from soil health to native plants. Community centers offer meeting spaces and bulletin boards, and often act as a bridge between individuals and grassroots projects. These are places where gardeners meet, share knowledge, trade resources, and build relationships that support long-term collaboration.

Purple Coneflower (*Echinacea purpurea*) and Blackfoot Daisy (*Melampodium leucanthum*) growing in the Lady Bird Johnson Wildflower Center in Austin, Texas.

How to Find Grants and Resources for Gardening Projects

Part of involvement in a sharing community is to participate in programs that support gardening and green initiatives. Grants, resources, and educational programs can exist specifically to support projects for residents who want to garden and reduce their overall costs. It could be for a community project like a pollinator garden, community food project, or neighborhood beautification effort, but it could also be available to an individual garden project. These resources and projects are also not only provided for those in economic need. Certainly that is one factor, but they have many other purposes as well. Awarding funding to individuals and groups could be to execute a political promise, build arts and culture, enrich neighborhoods, expand community knowledge, and gain awareness for environmental issues. Accessing and fulfilling these programs gives many benefits to the organization and community, and they will be grateful for your contributions.

Start by writing down a brainstorm about the project you want to find funding for. This will help you to get clear on what your needs are and sets the direction for the search.

Make a few notes in your garden journal on:

- What do you want to do? For example: *native pollinator garden, front-yard renovation, cutting garden, food growing.*
- Where is the location for the project (for example, renter's balcony, schoolyard, front lawn)?
- Why do you want to do the project (for example, neighborhood beautification, mental health, biodiversity)?
- Who benefits (for example, you, a specific neighborhood, kids, bees)?

Now, imagine you work for a nonprofit society and your job is to hunt for funding. Start your search online for local resources. Use search terms that list "[your project] + grant/funding/support [your city]." Here are some examples:

- [your neighborhood] grant [your city]
- pollinator garden funding [your region]
- front yard garden support [your town]
- native plant funding [your region]
- food garden grant [your town]
- community garden support [your city]

ASK DIRECTLY

Don't be afraid to reach out via phone or email to local garden stores, environmental nonprofits, or your city councilor or regional representative and ask for what you want. Keep your message short: Briefly explain your project and ask if they are donating plants or funds or know of any programs. Garden stores often have connections to manufacturers offering sponsorships, while nonprofits and elected officials frequently know about funding opportunities that aren't publicly advertised. This direct approach gets faster responses than lengthy proposals and you'll be surprised how successful it can be to simply ask.

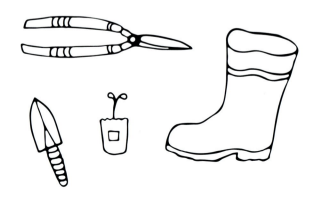

Researching Government and Municipal Programs

Government websites are treasure troves of information that many people overlook entirely. They often have projects dedicated to sustainability or environmental departments that offer grants, rebates, and incentive programs for residents and businesses. However, these funds can be largely unknown because they don't have big marketing budgets to get the word out to the public.

A bee border planted on the outer fence of a local community garden beautifies the neighborhood and attracts pollinators.

Programs range from simple rain barrel subsidies or tree planting initiatives to more involved energy efficiency upgrades and community garden projects. Don't just browse the main pages; dig into the planning and development sections, environmental services, and parks and recreation departments. Each may have its own pot of funding available.

Use the search bar on government websites for terms like: garden, rain barrel, rain garden, compost, grant, sponsorship, funding, project, and event. Or have a look through the specific branches:

- Utility companies provide rebates for water-wise landscaping, rain barrels, or shade tree planting.
- Watershed or stormwater management grants encourage gardens that reduce runoff and improve water quality.
- Public health departments sometimes fund gardens that support mental and physical well-being.
- Disaster recovery or climate adaptation funds support ecological restoration in areas impacted by fire, flood, or drought.
- National parks or urban green space initiatives encourage habitat creation and may partner with homeowners near green corridors.

Accessing Conservation Programs

Conservation authorities and local water boards are valuable resources that operate independently from municipal governments. These organizations have specific mandates to protect watersheds, prevent erosion, and promote sustainable land use practices. They often offer grants for projects that align with their conservation goals, such as native landscaping, stormwater management, habitat restoration, or agricultural best practices. The application processes are often less competitive than federal grants, and the staff at these organizations genuinely want to see projects succeed in their regions.

Search the term "conservation + [your city, town, or neighborhood] + grant/funding/sponsorship/program" to find projects in your area.

PROGRAM TYPES TO EXPLORE

Native plant societies may partner with municipalities to provide plants, education, or funds for rewilding residential areas with native plants.

Rewilding or biodiversity initiatives fund or support projects restoring native habitats and wild spaces.

Pollinator protection programs focus on creating pollinator habitat and may provide free seeds or small grants.

Habitat certification programs certify and support wildlife-friendly gardens, often with resources or discounts.

Climate action or carbon offset projects may offer funding for projects that sequester carbon or build climate resilience.

Opposite and above: An insect hotel and flowering comfrey at City Farmer, Compost Education Program. City Farmer is a community program in the Kitsilano neighborhood of Vancouver that has been teaching people how to grow food, compost, and become environmental stewards since 1978.

2

THE LOST ART OF HUNTING AND GATHERING: FINDING, FORAGING, AND REPURPOSING

Between houses, I moved into a rental property: a brand-new half-duplex with tall ceilings, gray-washed laminate floors, white walls, and black hardware. Everything was clean, white, and sterile. It was everything the modern-day design aesthetic told me was calming, yet something didn't sit right with me. It was lacking life. I brought in my plants in mismatched pots and set almost forty house-plants throughout the space. Then I brought in my furniture with warm wood tones and natural mate-rials. These pieces helped quite a lot, but somehow the rental was still not comforting. It remained sharp, angular, and cold on all six sides of the box that enclosed my family and things.

I was so glad to have spent 10 months inside that box, because the appeal from the outside was misleading. When house-hunting, I'd bounced between these new builds and century-old houses with architectural character. The new builds had modern-day conveniences like high-end appli-ances and open floor plans, efficiently packaged to maximize space. The old houses had scuffed wood floors, smallish separate rooms, outdated decora-tive features, and not nearly enough closets. And yet those old houses possessed a story and past that filled the space with life.

It was because of the time I had in the rental that I chose the house with character over the blank slate. I'm so glad I did. When I moved in, I had to embrace the quirks and oddities to figure out how to make it work for my family. The same applied to the outdoor spaces. The neglected gardens were mostly grass and overgrown shrubs, but it was from that foundation that I replanted, rewilded, and rejuvenated the land to grow my wild and free garden. That sterile square patch at the modern place could never become the garden of my dreams. But the garden at the heritage house has. I have met many neighbors as they stop by to chat about my designs, and as I sit here in my office writing this book, a woman hollered at me from the other side of the fence, "I love this sitting area, what a beautiful garden!"

She was referring to the sitting area in the middle of the cutting flower garden, originally just for a place to rest while cutting blooms. It's become such a welcoming spot that I'm constantly out there, having lunch, drinking coffee, and chat-ting with neighbors about plants, community, and politics. I love this space's uniqueness and how it's become part of me, helping me feel far more at ease than spaces designed for comfort through the modern aesthetic of perfection.

Opposite: A collection of unique terracotta pots adds the timeless style that was built over many years of treasure-hunting.

I planted a cutting garden around a small patio set for joy and connection. I use the table to make arrangements and it gets a new display depending on what's in bloom. I set extra bouquets on the fence for passersby to take home.

Finding Home in Uniqueness

It's dawned on me that what's more comforting than modern sterility is personalization. Somehow we've been fed a modern farmhouse aesthetic with motivational quotes on the walls and large open spaces. We're stripping away personality to decorate straight off a Pinterest board or an HGTV set. It's all whitewashed and meant to look serene, a supposed respite from the chaos of daily life. I'd argue that it's not the white walls and fluffed pillows that give us calm; it's surrounding ourselves with expressions of our inner desires. It's having the presence and aware-ness to live fully in the boldness and uniqueness that is you.

Finding your style isn't something that happens in a weekend. The charm, the magic, is in the hunt. There's something deeply satisfying about gath-ering materials over time, piece by piece, find by find. Joy comes from spotting that perfect stone for your garden path. Thrill arrives when you discover vintage garden tools at an estate sale that tell stories of gardens past. Excitement builds when trading plant cuttings with a neighbor, each carrying genetic histories unique to your community.

This hunting and gathering becomes a practice in patience, in delayed gratification. Unlike the instant satisfaction of filling a cart at a big-box store, collecting special pieces for your garden might take seasons, even years. Oh, but the stories they tell! The bench weathered by decades of rain that you restored by hand and the ceramic pot left in the bin behind that little studio you discovered on vacation; each item carries memories, connections, purpose.

This becomes harder and harder as companies find ways to reduce the barriers to shopping. There was a time when we wouldn't even consider buying things like clothing and live plants online and having them delivered to our homes. Now, the convenience seems to outweigh any uncertainties.

We've become so accustomed to a culture of *add to cart*, *one-click buying*, *next-day delivery*, and *free shipping* that the convenience often outweighs our concerns about quality.

Something more is lost in the act of instantaneous purchasing. The jokes about opening Amazon boxes and being surprised by their contents reflect a reality that's taken us away from our nature. We need fewer things and more time to source them. While a few retailers offering almost anything we could need makes it seem easier on the surface, the overall cost is much higher. We get less quality, create more waste, and lose the sense of success that comes from sourcing and acquiring materials needed to build our homes and lives, replacing them with the quick hit of impulse purchases.

I want to inspire you to live in your wildness, embracing what makes you come alive and gives you joy, not what's popular or standard or matches the current aesthetic of neutral everything. I want this to be your purest expression of heart and mind; a joyfulness that, when you see it, sparks the peace of feeling truly understood and seen in your space. Of course, this comes with some reprogramming. In this chapter, I'll present how we can find the materials we need by shopping our own shed, how to find space to garden if we don't have it readily available, and tips for sourcing used furniture, architectural salvage, reclaimed wood, and hardscaping materials.

Flower pots chosen with care and intention will never go out of style.

The Artist's Garden

Susan Lee's Vancouver garden showcases the path to gardens that truly nourish not just the land, but our souls through beauty, art, and intention. The bronze garden sculptures were made by her son and add focal points among reclaimed materials. The arbors, plant supports, and pathways have been built over time with found materials. The garden is full of color from spring through fall with an abundance of flowering shrubs, vines, and perennials that surround the entertaining area.

Sculptures 'Breaking Monument' (opposite) and 'Locavore' (top right) are by artist Benjamin Lee (www.instagram.com/howearthly)

First, Shop Your Shed

A garden shed is a beautiful thing; at least it has the potential to be. In theory, it's a place where tools are easy to find, pots are stacked neatly, and supplies are right where you need them. In reality? It's all too easy to end up with a jumble of half-empty bags of soil, forgotten projects, and that one broken tool you swear you'll fix "someday."

But a well-organized shed isn't just about aesthetics; it makes gardening easier and more enjoyable. If your shed is a cluttered disaster zone, you'll probably avoid it, wasting time searching for things or, worse, rebuying what you already have buried in there somewhere. But if your shed is tidy, functional, and (dare I say) inviting, you'll be more likely to use what you have and actually enjoy the space.

CONSCIOUS PURCHASES

When my son rushes in, excited to spend his entire month's allowance on a toy he already owns six versions of, I gently remind him to check his toy box first. I get it. Newness is certainly tempting, and applying that same restraint when I see new bypass pruners online takes real strength. I know I have four pairs in the garden shed, but they're rusty and need sharpening. While it's tempting to purchase the new ones and toss the old, it's in these moments that we take control of our consumption, making the smart decision to delay the gratification of that impulsive purchase and use what we already have.

WHAT TO KEEP VS. WHAT TO LET GO

Some things are worth hanging onto. Rusty tools? They can be cleaned and sharpened. Broken terra-cotta pots? Perfect for a charming bit of garden art. Wood scraps? Ideal for last-minute trellises or compost bin repairs. And let's not forget the ever-versatile plastic nursery pots that can be used for holding seedlings, plant divisions, and your garden glove collection.

Then, there are the things that have officially outlived their usefulness, like cracked plastic pots, expired products, leaking bottles of mystery liquid, and anything moldy or pest-infested. I'm sure all of this goes without saying. You can also reconsider how many duplicates you need. If you have six pairs of bypass pruners but only ever use three, consider sharing the extras with your local gardening group to make sure they get to fulfill their destiny rather than just rusting away.

Keep:
- Old tools that can be repaired or revived
- Wood scraps and pallets
- Metal stakes and sticks that can be used for staking plants
- Metal or plastic jars and tins with lids (no glass)
- Old furniture and shelving that can be repurposed in the garden
- Twine, wire, zip ties, and hardware odds and ends
- Old clothes and fabric scraps

Let Go Of:
- Broken items beyond repair
- Expired chemicals and synthetic fertilizers
- Moldy or pest-infested materials
- Stuff you haven't touched in years
- Excess nursery pots
- Too many duplicates

MANAGE THE SHED

The best way to keep a shed useful is to stay on top of the mess before it takes over. Set up a system that works for you. Not some picture-perfect Pinterest version, but something practical that makes sense for how you actually use your space.

Do:

✓ **Put things back where they belong.** Taking an extra minute to return something to its spot saves you from tearing apart the whole shed next time you need it.

✓ **Use matching bins.** Not only does this keep things looking neat, but it also stops you from playing Tetris with odd-shaped containers every time you tidy up.

✓ **Install a bin rack.** If your bins are stacked on top of each other, you will avoid using them. A simple shelf or rack makes it so much easier to grab what you need.

✓ **Choose clear bins and labels.** No one has time to open five different containers just to find the garden twine.

✓ **Keep frequently used items up front.** The stuff you use daily? Keep it easy to reach. The Christmas lights? They can stay in the back until December.

✓ **Have a junk bin.** Random bits and bobs accumulate no matter what. A dedicated place for them is the first place you'll look when you need them and saves time trying to figure out where they should be stored.

✓ **Keep a binder for important papers.** Tool manuals, plant tags, receipts, and notes can be stored together in the shed. Attach a hole punch and pen to the binder and add some pocket dividers so you can quickly add new papers.

✓ **Plan for a twice-a-year cleanup.** It will get a bit out of hand, but that can be handled in spring cleaning (and fall).

✓ **Make it feel like a space worth caring for.** A little decoration, a nice workbench, even a favorite sign: It all helps you see your shed as a space that deserves attention, not just a dumping ground.

Don't:

✗ **Put wet or dirty things in the shed.** They'll end up moldy and rusty.

✗ **Let cobwebs take over.** It's quite unpleasant to have to swipe through them to access your things.

✗ **Store things that can rot.** This should go without saying.

✗ **Pile up equipment in the way.** You don't want to climb over a lawnmower just to grab a trowel.

✗ **Toss things mindlessly.** Before throwing something out, ask yourself: *Can it be reused, repaired, or donated?*

✗ **Rush decisions.** Not sure if you need to keep that pile of nursery pots? Set them aside for a bit instead of making a snap decision you'll regret later.

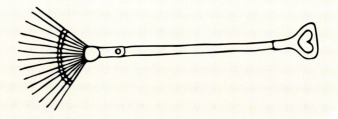

THE WILD & FREE GARDEN

The Posh Potting House

Delphia Johnstone's potting house was lovingly built by her husband, Bob, so that she would have a place to drink champagne with her friends while potting up her collection of over 300 hostas. It features a large built-in countertop with a grate to sweep soil into a bin below, an organized collection of her garden tools, and a beautiful view of the garden.

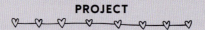

outdoor solar chandelier

This DIY solar chandelier light was made with materials found in my garden shed and took no more than fifteen minutes to put together. Since then, it has become one of the most-loved decorative objects in the garden. It adds a whimsical touch hanging from a tree above a rustic table-and-chair set.

MATERIALS:

- Wire hanging basket frame with chains
- Outdoor stake solar light
- Beads, shells, or chandelier crystals

MAKE IT!

1. Source a hanging basket that has a round circle of wire at the bottom. This will be used to hold the solar light.

2. Source a solar light that will sit in the hole without needing to be glued or adjusted in any way. Standard stake lights that line pathways are inexpensive and will fit well in this project.

3. Turn the basket so that it is convex and reattach the chains to the top wires around the hole.

4. Decorate the chandelier with whatever materials you can find. Old chandelier crystals are easy to find at architectural salvage stores, but you can also find free materials at the beach, such as shells and beach glass.

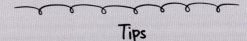

Tips

A solar light works best when charged in direct sun, but I prefer charging it in ambient light because it will only glow for an hour after sunset, which is perfect for evening garden enjoyment. New lights perform better than old ones, but you can learn to replace the solar battery at a repair clinic or online.

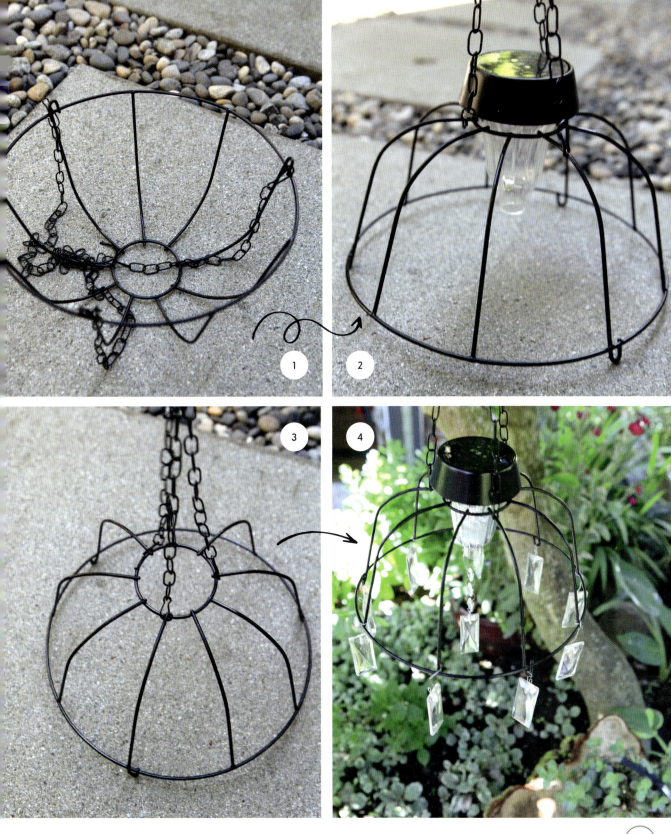

Colorful paint makes for a quick way to refresh furniture for outdoors.

Find Quality Outdoor Furniture for Free

In the world of secondhand goods, the harder something is to move or store, the better deal you'll get. Throw in seasonal usefulness, and outdoor furniture is some of the most valuable secondhand finds available for free or very close to free.

In many cases, people lack adequate winter storage, especially in urban neighborhoods. This means you can snag some great deals and plenty of giveaways in the late summer and fall that people simply can't store. Year-round, you can find furniture being rehomed when people move, redecorate, or renovate. People also discard items because they're becoming weathered. It's expected that outdoor items get dirty, start to break down, or need some refinishing after a few seasons, but some people prefer to replace rather than repair. Having basic repair and maintenance skills means you can use just a little elbow grease to save yourself a bundle.

Search for pieces in salvageable condition to make sure they're not going to cost you more time or effort than they are worth. Consider whether wooden items can be easily sanded or stained because these jobs are not difficult, but skip furniture with warped, cracked, or broken wood. For glass, concrete, or wicker items that have dirt or build up, they might just need pressure washing or a good scrub to restore them. Get yourself a stiff brush or borrow a pressure washer to clean them up.

CHOOSING OUTDOOR FURNITURE TO RESTORE

All outdoor furniture needs maintenance, and someone's lack of desire to maintain their furniture could equal your chance to pick it up for free.

For **wood**, first check to make sure it doesn't have large cracks and isn't rotting or warped because these things are difficult to repair. If the wood is in good condition and just needs refinishing, it's fairly easy to sand it down and refinish with paint, exterior stain, and then a weatherproof sealant topcoat.

Metal, like wrought iron, aluminum, or steel, is commonly used for outdoor furniture. Metal usually lasts well outdoors, but when you notice significant rust or corrosion, I'd give it a pass. If it just needs a bit of refinishing, you can sand any rusty spots, clean the metal thoroughly, and apply rust-resistant paint.

Wicker is also common for outdoor furniture, either natural or resin. The quality of resin wicker varies greatly and often can't be replaced. If you see wicker unwinding and broken, it's a bigger job to restore, so only pick this up if you want to practice your wicker refurbishing skills. If the wicker is just dirty but still in good condition, all it needs is a solid cleaning.

Plastic and resin, similar to wicker, can vary greatly in quality. I have high-end garden pots that have lasted 12 years and still look brand new, while other plastic pots deteriorated within one season. Look for products made to last so you're not contributing to single-use plastic waste. Good quality plastic won't fade, crack, or warp, and only needs cleaning with soap and water.

Glass tabletops are simple to clean, but avoid any with chips or cracks.

Concrete and stone are long-lasting materials that clean up nicely with a pressure washer. Avoid any that are chipped or broken unless that's the look you're going for.

Design with Color

Bold colors are a high-impact, low-cost way to elevate outdoor spaces. They add personality, create focal points, and make even simple items feel intentional and stylish. Add paint to a wall, bench, or gate, or add pops of color with annuals. This also applies to the vegetables you grow. Nothing says "homegrown" like gold and purple cherry tomatoes garnishing a Bloody Mary.

Repurposing Furniture Finds into Stylish Garden Features

The most creative gardens I've toured all had one thing in common: They reimagined indoor furniture, giving it a second life as a garden feature. I'm not suggesting you move a brand-new solid wood dining table out to your patio, unless of course the table was picked up for free on the curbside. If someone is discarding it and you happen to be the lucky person to find it, then set about weatherproofing it and let it be the star of your yard.

Our own castoffs can be turned into something useful outside in the garden. A broken mirror becomes a focal point when succulents and moss fill in the cracks. An old hutch transforms into a potting bench with character, its shelves perfect for storing tools and supplies. A clawfoot bathtub makes a wonderful garden fountain, its vintage curves adding elegance to any corner.

Not every piece needs a complete makeover to earn its place outdoors. Sometimes the charm lies in letting weather do its work. Chippy paint, rust stains, and worn edges speak of years lived and stories accumulated. These imperfections become features rather than flaws when moved to the garden setting.

Turning indoor castoffs into outdoor treasures requires creativity, weatherproofing, and drainage holes. Start with sturdy solid wood or metal frames that can handle the elements. Look past ugly paint jobs and torn upholstery to examine the structure underneath. Is it level? Are the joints tight? Will it stand the test of time? A solidly built piece will outlast both weather and your weekend project enthusiasm, becoming a permanent part of your garden's character.

The Vintage Garden

Sue Bath's North Vancouver garden features eighty chandeliers hanging from the trees, metal bed frames turned into garden beds complete with flowers and moss, a vintage chair that has become a piece of living art, and many other treasures. The fountain she made out of an old iron clawfoot tub is a whimsical play on her name as she has personally found and installed all of the art around her garden.

vintage trailer guest house

Lola is my guest house. She's a gorgeous 1963 Aristocrat Lo-Liner Travel Trailer I bought from a woman named Norma in Alberta. Norma collected vintage trailers and restored them. She had a whole fleet of beautiful aluminum trailers, each painted a different color and given its own name: Happy, Pearl, Lola, and several others. These trailers were absolutely charming, restored in that perfect vintage style that brings peace and joy, enveloping you like a grandma's hug.

I love Lola for her vintage charm, but she's also a practical way of increasing my space and beautifying my backyard. In a small home, with a small lot (and no storage like a garage or shed), I had to be creative in my backyard design. I wanted a place that could be used as an office or guest house, and building a permanent structure requires expense, time, expertise, and permits. A vintage trailer made sense as the least expensive and most stylish way to give me the extra space I needed.

Lola embodies wild and free design: rescuing something with bones and character from a bygone era rather than buying new. There's something deeply satisfying about restoring quality craftsmanship that time has seasoned, reducing waste while creating a space that feels authentically lived-in from day one. If you're looking for an economical solution for a stylish backyard feature that acts as a cozy place for guests to stay, supplemental party space, extra storage, and a quiet retreat to work in, a vintage trailer delivers on all fronts.

This little guest house becomes a charming getaway right on your property. It looks beautiful in the yard, adds a unique theme to your space, and frankly looks nicer than having a garage. When not hosting guests, it serves as the perfect spot for a quiet cup of tea or a private conversation; a little retreat just steps from your back door.

SITE PREPARATION:

1. Measure your trailer carefully to ensure you create an adequately sized pad with a few feet of clearance on all sides.

2. Clear and level the ground where the trailer will sit. Also clear and level the area to the road.

3. Consider access; you may need to modify fencing or create a gate wide enough to maneuver the trailer in. Backing up a trailer is a skill that takes some practice.

4. Cover the area with bark mulch or create a more permanent pad if desired.

SETTING UP THE TRAILER:

1. Move the trailer into position (you'll likely need help with this).

2. Use leveling jacks to stabilize it in place.

3. Add blocks behind the wheels to prevent movement.

4. Add a portable set of steps for easy access to the door.

5. Connect power from your house for lights and electricity.

6. Set up the interior with bedding, table linens, and any desired furnishings.

7. Store camping gear and seasonal items in the trunk or under benches when not in use.

MAKE A SPACE

To make space for Lola, I replaced two 8-foot (2.4 m) cedar fence panels with new ones spaced wider apart and fitted them with swing gate hardware. Now I could back the trailer right in from the alley.

MAINTENANCE TIPS:

- Ensure the trailer is completely waterproofed (water damage is the biggest threat to a travel trailer because it can bring rot and mold).
- Seal all windows and edges to prevent leaks.
- Consider installing an arbor over the trailer for protection.
- At a minimum, cover with a tarp when not in use and over the rainy or snowy months.
- Have all propane appliances and electrical systems professionally inspected.
- In wet climates, run a small heater at 50°F (10°C) during winter to prevent mold.

To prepare the land, I leveled out the grass and weeds, cut back some trees, and evened out the space. You could certainly build a permanent concrete pad, but because I wasn't sure how long I'd keep the trailer there, I simply covered the leveled area with bark mulch before driving the trailer in.

Architectural Salvage: Finding Treasures for Free

I have a photographer friend who shoots only the most exceptionally beautiful homes for design magazines. We were chatting one day about what it takes to get a feature spread in one of these magazines because it's the question she hears most. Her answer is always the same: You've got to hunt for the good stuff. Something special. Something with soul. Estate sales; demo houses; garage sales in older neighborhoods; thrift stores; salvage yards, especially architectural salvage yards: Those are the treasure troves.

After you find something truly unique, the fun really begins. Transform found items into something unexpected: arbors, trellises, wall art, fences, and showpieces that become the highlight of your garden.

I love trellises and arbors made from old iron gates or bits of decorative architecture that have stood the test of time. You never quite know what you're going to find, and that's part of the joy. The best gardens aren't built with a plan from the store. They're built from stories and salvage and serendipity.

Above: If you look closely at this outdoor table, you'll see it was repurposed from a bowling alley floor. The markings give it character and casters on the steel frame give it portability. It serves as outdoor dining next to built-in benches covered in blankets, pillows, and sheepskins to cozy up the space. Opposite: Recycled lumber could be used to make a planter bench to frame the entertaining space.

Reclaimed Wood: Repurposing Discarded Lumber

There are a few types of wood you'll see repeatedly in outdoor projects. Hardwoods like cedar or antique lumber are ideal for outdoor use. Softer woods like pine don't hold up the same way in the garden. If you're building something structural that needs to last, choose wood that's naturally rot-resistant.

Cedar is an outdoor favorite because it has natural oils that protect it from fungi and bacteria, so it breaks down much more slowly than other types of wood. Both Western red and yellow varieties of cedar work wonderfully, as do redwood, black locust, and white oak. Teak is often found in outdoor furniture because it is extremely durable, but it also comes with a hefty price tag. Pressure-treated wood, often used in framing like under decks, was once treated with chromated-copper arsenate (CCA), a preservative to resist rot. You can usually spot it from a slight greenish hue or small slits in the wood where chemicals were injected. It's sturdy, but not something you want near food plants.

That's the catch with salvaged wood: You often don't know where it's been. Years ago, I found some old railway ties, 150 years old, and wanted to use them to build veggie beds. I researched what they were treated with and found they were safe (and had clearly stood the test of time). But it's a risk if you don't know the wood's history.

If you're picking up wood from demolition sites, salvage yards, architectural reclamation spots, Habitat for Humanity stores, or even from a back alley, think twice before putting it in your garden. Unless you're certain it's untreated, avoid use in food gardens at minimum. Check for paint that might contain lead or toxins or avoid painted wood unless you know it's safe. Look for signs of rot or pest infestation that could spread to your garden.

PALLET WOOD

Pallets are another source for inexpensive (sometimes free) wood. They used to be everywhere, but thanks to their popularity, they're harder to find now or you'll need to pay a few dollars. When looking for pallet wood, aim for those that haven't been treated or stamped with mystery codes. Skip anything that's rotted or splintered beyond repair.

Most pallets are made from softwoods like spruce and pine, or sometimes oak. They won't last forever outdoors, but they're great for planters, benches, garden furniture, and other creative projects. Disassembling pallets takes some effort, but once you get the hang of it, you can get a surprising amount of usable lumber from each one.

PALLET WOOD TIPS

- Use a pallet buster tool if you disassemble often. It makes the job so much easier by applying even pressure and saving your back.
- Choose "HT" pallets. Pallets marked with "HT" have been heat-treated to eliminate pests without the use of chemicals, making them safe for indoor projects and garden use. Pallets marked with "MB" have been treated with methyl bromide, which has been banned in some countries and should be avoided for use in home gardens.
- If boards are cracked or damaged, cut them down into smaller useful pieces for signs, small shelves, or planters.

CARING FOR OUTDOOR WOOD

With proper care, garden structures built from quality reclaimed wood will last for many years while adding natural warmth and character to your garden space. On an annual basis:

- Clean with mild soap and water, but never pressure wash because it damages the wood surface.
- Check for cracks, rot, or loose joints. Ensure good drainage and elevation from soil to extend the wood's life.
- Sand and reseal areas as needed.

Natural Weathering: Cedar and redwood develop a beautiful silvery patina when left untreated. This approach requires no maintenance, though untreated wood won't last quite as long as sealed wood.

Natural Sealants: Apply natural oils, eco-friendly wood treatments, or water-based sealers for protection without harsh chemicals.

Exterior Stains: Choose nontoxic, exterior-grade options that penetrate and protect the wood.

Shou Sugi Ban: This Japanese woodburning technique chars the surface of the wood, creating a protective layer that resists water, insects, and decay. The charred wood is then brushed and sealed with oil.

A BACKYARD SPA OASIS MADE FROM RECLAIMED MATERIALS

This backyard transformation proves that luxury doesn't require new materials. Found on Facebook Marketplace, this spa was being given away—including the hot tub, wood gazebo, and outdoor shower—for the trade of the labor to remove it. It was built from recycled film set materials by a carpenter who understood the value of repurposing. Because he was moving from his rental, the landlord wanted it removed. Originally, he listed the spa for sale, but the price came down as he approached his move date.

Rather than letting these materials end up in a landfill, I quickly arranged to disassemble the structure and transport everything to my backyard. The gazebo dimensions did not fit my space, so I reconfigured the design. The space transformed into a natural oasis, with the open-beam roof providing a view of my neighbor's majestic Douglas fir above and dappled light perfect for surrounding shade plants. Large pots filled with ferns, hostas, and seasonal indoor plants make the reclaimed materials feel integrated into the landscape. The Japanese shou sugi ban woodburning technique on the cedar privacy walls creates a striking charcoal finish that naturally resists weather while highlighting the wood grain.

For the trade of labor, I was able to access a working spa for a nominal price, keeping it from entering the waste cycle. While a hot tub may seem to be a wasteful use of water, I no longer bathe indoors, using far less water overall. I improved the insulation to hold heat efficiently and use wind-generated electricity rather than natural gas to power it. This is a perfect example of how one person's discards can become the foundation for sustainable luxury when approached with creativity and environmental consciousness.

Bamboo poles and willow whips are great branches to use in the garden.

Driftwood and large branches can be a focal point, anchoring the garden with a natural piece of art.

Foraging for Branches and Sticks

Branches and sticks provide excellent building materials for garden supports and structures. Strong branches work perfectly as primary supports, while decorative bentwood can be woven around them to create climbing structures for plants. Straight, thick branches make ideal trellises for peas, beans, clematis, and other climbing plants. Thin, flexible branches can be woven into wreath forms, baskets, and living fences.

Gather branches from your own garden or contact arborists and municipal landscaping crews, who often have excess material available. If all else fails, forage responsibly from wild spaces where collecting branches is permitted.

Look for straight, sturdy branches with diameters between ½ inch to 2 inches (1.3 to 5 cm), depending on your project needs. For weaving projects, seek flexible branches like willow or hazel. For strength and stability, select hardwoods like maple, alder, or fruit tree prunings. Fresh or recently cut branches work best. Branches that are past their prime are too brittle.

Bring sharp pruners or loppers, gloves, and a collection bin. Do not cut branches from living trees. Look for recently fallen wood and skip anything rotted, insect infested, or fungus covered. Wear long sleeves, long pants, and closed-toe shoes with sturdy soles for protection.

Strip off side shoots, leaves, and thorns, then cut branches to needed lengths. Let green wood cure in a shady, dry spot for a few days unless you're bending it. Fresh wood is the best for bending projects. Install supports at least 6 to 8 inches (15 to 20 cm) deep in the garden for stability, using a mallet to drive them in.

Check local regulations because many beaches, forests, and parks prohibit wood collection. Take only what you need, never over-harvest, and leave plenty for wildlife. The goal is gentle, respectful harvesting that maintains the natural ecosystem.

Kimmy Andrews and Gerald Hannig in North Saanich, BC, sustainably collect driftwood to make Christmas Trees as gifts during the holidays.

PRESSURE-FIT TRELLIS

To make a pressure-fit trellis with branches, measure the height and width that you need and make sure that you have branches that are that height for the vertical branches and that width for the horizontal branches. Start by staking the end of one of the vertical branches into the ground and stake the remaining branches 6 to 12 inches (15 to 30 cm) apart until you've reached the desired length. Then, use the horizontal branches and weave them through the stakes by passing them alternately behind and in front of each of the stakes. Slide the pole down through the stakes to about 6 inches (15 cm) from the bottom and continue this process until you have a sturdy trellis that has the spacing that you need for your plants.

Making the Most of Autumn Leaves

When neighbors bag their fall leaves for municipal collection, you're looking at free composting gold. Dried leaves provide an ideal balance for compost (roughly one-third nitrogen and two-thirds carbon) without needing additional ingredients. Add them to your compost bin or set them in a pile at the back of the garden to compost.

You can also use leaves to mulch garden beds in the fall. They'll decompose naturally over a few years, but you can speed the process by chopping them into leaf mold with a lawnmower or leaf blower in reverse. Come spring, simply move leaves aside for emerging plants or let established plants grow through them. Top with a couple of inches of compost to accelerate breakdown. There's no need to remove the leaf layer completely.

Before collecting a neighbor's leaves, knock on their door and ask for permission, and find out what's in the bags. Politely ask if they used pesticides or herbicides, had evidence of pests or disease, or mixed any possible invasive species in. If you're unsure about any of the answers, leave the leaves behind.

FREE MULCH

There are websites (like ChipDrop) that help gardeners who want wood chips meet arborists and tree services who are trying to get rid of them. If there isn't an active program like this in your neighborhood, call around to local tree companies, because they often have wood chips to give away.

Left: Long-lasting natural stone can often be given away in trade for the labor of removing them. Right: There's something deeply satisfying about building the bones of your outdoor space with materials that have contrast and history. A chimney whose bricks became garden steps gives this renovated garden a touch of its 100-year-old history.

Recycling Hardscapes: Pathways, Patios, and Stepping Stones

Used hardscape materials are easy to come by as long as you are approaching your project with flexibility. It can be one of the most fun and creative parts of building the foundation for your garden. The key is layering different textures and materials: stone slabs paired with weathered bricks, river stones nestled against gravel, and cement pavers creating geometric patterns that guide visitors through your space. Creative hardscaping gives your space some interest, while not making you wholly dependent on finding a certain square footage of one type of material.

Used hardscape material can be found for low or no cost, often in return for the labor of removal. Look for materials that are easy to disassemble and load, as the labor cost of removal increases dramatically if the materials are not easy to access. Dirty stones can be easily cleaned with a hose or pressure washer and look as good as new once cleaned and installed.

Garden bricks are concrete blocks shaped like traditional bricks, usually simple rectangles, but sometimes available in decorative shapes for walkways or patios.

Reclaimed clay bricks often salvaged from old chimneys or demolition sites, have great character, but are fragile outdoors. Hollow bricks can't support much weight, and clay bricks crack and crumble when water freezes inside them.

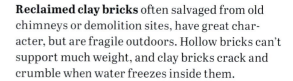

Natural stone is very pricey new, so snap up free flagstone, slate, and bluestone. Choose slabs at least 2 to 3 inches (5 to 8 cm) thick for walkways to prevent cracking under foot traffic and lay a gravel base for stability.

Broken concrete, also known as "Urbanite," is easy to find for free because it's expensive to dispose of. Use it in place of flagstone for natural-looking patios or paths. The irregular shapes create fun puzzle-piece installations.

Concrete patio pavers are available in countless shapes and sizes. Garden renovators frequently leave them stacked curbside for free pickup. Large 24 x 24-inch (61 x 61 cm) slabs work perfectly for shed bases or quick patios.

Gravel or crushed stone works as a base layer under other materials or fills entire areas for permeable patios.

Wood rounds and pallet slats create rustic pathways, but become slippery in damp, mossy conditions and are not as long-lasting as stone. Composite is longer lasting and can often be found second hand for small projects like bridges.

River stones are refined, rounded gravel that creates a Zen-garden aesthetic. These stones look beautiful in dry creek beds or minimalist spaces.

PATIO VS. STEPPING STONE SITE PREPARATION

Hardscapes like dry riverbeds, patios, stepping stones, and lawns with embedded pathways have installation requirements that will make the difference between a beautiful, lasting installation and one that becomes a maintenance headache. The key to any successful hardscape project is proper preparation. Without it, you'll end up with broken and unlevel tripping hazards as opposed to a welcoming and safe place to walk. If you have ever seen a patio where the bricks or pavers are uneven or seem to be sinking, that's a sign of improper site preparation.

DON'T USE GRAVEL AND SAND TO LEVEL STEPPING STONES IN GARDENS AND LAWNS

Using gravel and sand to level stepping stones in gardens and lawns can cause more harm than good. Some sand is fine to use in lawn applications, but keep both sand and gravel out of the garden beds. These materials can disrupt healthy soil, interfere with drainage, and make future adjustments more diffi-cult as the ground shifts. Instead, just level the soil beneath each stone and backfill with native soil, mulch, or grass.

Large Patio

1. Measure and mark your area.
2. Dig out the entire space 7 to 9 inches (18 to 23 cm) deep.
3. Frame the perimeter with wood or a retaining wall, if needed.
4. Level and tamp down the soil.
5. Line the area with permeable landscape fabric.
6. Add 4 to 6 inches (10 to 15 cm) of ¾-inch (1.9 cm) crushed gravel, in 2-inch (5 cm) layers, tamping each layer.
7. Add 1 inch (2.5 cm) of concrete sand.
8. Screed the sand level with a straight edge like a 2x4 (3.8 x 8.9 cm).
9. Set pavers into the sand bed.
10. Sweep sand into the joints.

Stepping Stones

1. Dig out an area matching each stone's size.
2. Level the soil in each hole.
3. Set the stone and adjust the soil underneath until level.
4. Position slightly above grass level for lawn areas and position flush with mulch level for garden areas.
5. Fill in soil around stepping stones and seed or much.

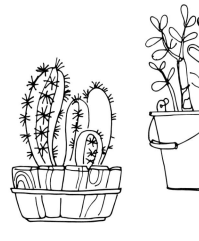

build a dry riverbed garden

Living in a rainforest teaches you the true purpose of rain gardens: returning water to the land where it falls. It's about more than just managing a high water table or unpredictable atmospheric river events. It's about accommodating the changes in water delivered to the garden due to increasing periods of drought and other seasonal changes that require more resilience. The more we remove the rainwater from our roofs into gutters and downspouts that cycle back to the sewers rather than the land, the more we need to bring in supplemental water to our gardens. From an ecological perspective, this affects our local public spaces like marshes and creeks.

Standing in my waterlogged front yard, I saw opportunity instead of problems. Rather than directing that water into city drains, I chose to filter it through the soil to feed the surrounding plants. I built a dry riverbed that functions as both drainage system and pathway through what became a thriving wildflower meadow.

In practice, this dry river design is a simple solution to reduce ongoing water management. In months where there are heavy rains, it drains quickly and keeps water away from the house. In times of drought, no supplemental water is needed. The wildflowers basically take care of themselves and look gorgeous doing it.

This shift in thinking, from fighting water to partnering with it, changes everything. You have the power to transform problems into solutions that work with nature's systems instead of against them.

MATERIALS:

- Shovel
- Water-permeable landscape fabric
- Small and large river rocks
- Longer downspouts or drainage extensions
- Scissors or utility knife (for cutting landscape fabric)
- Natural paver stones for stable walking areas (optional)

1. Assess the area for drainage problems. Choose a location where water naturally collects but is safely away from the house foundation.

2. Extend downspouts or redirect runoff to the planned dry riverbed location to move water away from structures and toward the garden.

3. Outline the shape of the dry riverbed with a hose, rope, or flour. A natural, winding shape looks best and helps water flow effectively.

4. Dig a shallow trench along the outline. The depth can vary depending on how much water needs to be managed, but generally 6 to 12 inches (15 to 30 cm) deep is sufficient.

5. Lay down water-permeable landscape fabric in the trench and cover with river stones.

6. Continue to add river stones with smaller 1 to 2-inch (2.5 to 5 cm) rocks on the inner part of the river and larger 4-inch (10 cm) or larger size rocks on the edges for a natural look.

The dry river handles extra water during rains, keeps moisture in the soil for nearby plants, and makes a charming path through the garden. Maintenance is minimal: occasionally trim back overgrown plants along the edges and adjusting stones if needed. If you want a more stable path for regular walking, you can add stepping stones.

Creating the dry river solved the drainage problem, protected the house from excess moisture, gave the garden a beautiful feature, and made it easier to walk through the wildflower lawn without damaging it.

a stepping stone patio in an afternoon

The fundamental difference between patio and stepping stone installation is the number of units used in the build. Large patios, driveways, and paths require comprehensive site preparation no matter the size of paver you use. The base requires excavation, framing, proper drainage layers of gravel and sand, and systematic paver placement to handle foot traffic and weather. Stepping stones, on the other hand, are individual installations where you dig pockets in the garden or lawn. These don't require frames or a gravel and sand base.

It's not always necessary to lay the landscaping plans out in stone to plant your garden. A garden design can grow as organically as the flowers and vegetables we have in our yards. As the plants fill in spaces and the garden evolves, spaces can emerge that call for pathways and patios.

Patios require a foundation that won't fail, while stepping stones create perfectly placed landing spots that you'll inevitably need to adjust every few years as they settle. Using this logic, if you want to create a small patio with large pavers, you can build a naturalistic stepping stone patio that fits right into the garden.

THE BASE

A brick patio would need to have a level base of crushed gravel and sand, tamped and leveled to set the bricks in. Organically shaped stepping stones, however, are much more forgiving. Treated as temporary hardscaping, larger pieces of rock or concrete can be set directly on soil. The ideal size for stepping stones is between 12–24 inches (30–61 cm) so they're wide enough to hold the weight of a person or furniture without sinking into the soil, but also not so big that they could crack from soil-level changes below.

MATERIALS:

- Shovel
- Large paving stones, 12 to 24 inches (30 to 61 cm) in width
- 6-foot (1.8 cm) 2x4 (3.8 x 8.9 cm) lumber
- Landscape tamper

1. Mark the space that borders the patio by digging a perimeter with the shovel. Then, dig out the garden soil or turf grass to the depth of the paving stones. For instance, if the paving stones are 2 inches (5 cm) thick, then dig the hole 2 inches (5 cm) down.

2. Use the lumber as a screed rail to level the soil. Start at one edge and pull the board across the soil to level it. Gently slope the grade away from any buildings. Tamp the soil down firmly with a tamper. This step ensures that the patio will not sink over time. In a small area with compacted soil, you can flood the area with water, then stomp on it instead to compact the soil.

3. Lay out the stepping stones in the pattern that you like, keeping the gaps as small as possible.

4. Backfill the patio stones with soil and sweep it into the crevices. Seed a groundcover or plant moss between the stones for a natural look.

MAINTENANCE

Every few years, the patio stones may need to be lifted again by removing them from the soil, adding more soil in low spots, and tamping it down. Weeding between the pavers may also be necessary throughout the growing season.

3

FREE PLANTS THROUGH SEEDS AND PROPAGATION

I clearly remember the moment I became a propagatrix. Early in my gardening journey, I'd read that heirloom tomatoes produce seeds that grow true to type, preserving their parent's exact characteristics. This discovery sent me straight to the farmer's market, where I bought the most beautiful specimens of each variety, brought them home for tasting, then carefully scooped out their seeds for fermentation in mason jars.

Following the instructions precisely, I lined up all those jars on my windowsill. When the mold appeared, I felt simultaneously horrified and delighted, excited that my little science experiment was actually working. After fermentation completed, I scraped off the moldy layer, strained and dried the seeds, then stored them in labeled envelopes for winter. The next year I started the seeds, transplanted them to my garden, and dove headfirst into learning about heirloom tomatoes. I made some classic beginner mistakes like starting the plants too early, providing insufficient light, and waiting too long to pot them up. I still harvested plenty of tomatoes that summer and gained invaluable experience.

That adventure hooked me on propagation. After two decades of experimenting, I know what actually works: nature. Plants want to reproduce, and one of the ways they encourage us humans to help them is by producing tasty fruit or gorgeous flowers that we fall so in love with that we just have to have more! You thought you were in control here? Think again. Your free will was never in play. Plants have been enticing us since we first joined them on this Earth, so it's with a dash of humility and reverence for nature that we "help" them reproduce.

Lucky for us, plants have made this partnership pretty straightforward. In this chapter, we'll explore the different propagation methods like seed starting, division, and cuttings. While every plant has its quirks and preferences, the instructions show techniques for you to practice. Even more, you will see how easy it is to propagate plants. While you may also make some great mistakes, the risk is low and the end reward will be new knowledge and a collection of free plants.

Opposite: A prolific, perennial herb garden started from seeds and cuttings. The Yuzu tree was a gift from a friend who saved the seeds from a fruit.

WHAT IS PROPAGATION?

Propagation is our intentional participation in creating the next generation of plants rather than leaving everything to natural biological processes. It covers seed starting, cuttings, grafting, and division. Plants reproduce on their own through sexual or asexual reproduction, which we call *natural reproduction*. The magic of *propagation* happens when humans step in to guide, encourage, or speed up the process. It's how gardeners participate in the plant life cycle, giving plants a helpful nudge to grow and multiply.

Sunflower seeds are best to mature on the plant, however it's a race to get them before the birds or squirrels do.

Shake it up! Poppy seeds are ready to harvest when you can hear them rattle inside the pod. These tiny maracas also make a charming addition to flower arrangements.

Saving and Sharing Seeds

Saving seeds is a time-honored tradition that used to be the core of gardening and farming. For many generations, gardeners carefully selected seeds from the healthiest and most productive plants to ensure the strongest plants in future years. These practices not only preserved the genetics, but allowed those plants to thrive naturally and adapt to local conditions. Today, things have changed dramatically. Commercial seeds, especially those used in agriculture, are often patented hybrids or genetically modified organisms (GMOs). Because of intellectual property laws, saving and replanting seeds from these varieties is considered a violation of the patent. Farmers can face legal action or fines, even when the patented seeds were unintentionally "planted" through cross-pollination or wind drift. What was once a common practice rooted in sustainability and self-reliance has become legally risky, forcing many growers to buy new seeds every season instead of saving their own.

Thankfully, saving seeds is not a political issue for the home gardener. The practice is simple, inexpensive, and worth adding to your seasonal garden schedule. Here are the common methods used to save seeds.

This species tulip produces plenty of seeds in an attractive pod, however it will take 3-4 years for the seeds to grow into large enough bulbs to flower. Allow them to self-seed in a place where you have the patience to let them naturalize. Or remove the flowers before they bloom to send the energy back to the bulb to overwinter.

FLOWERS TO COLLECT AND SOW

- Calendula (*Calendula officinalis*)
- Zinnia (*Zinnia elegans*)
- Marigold (*Tagetes* spp.)
- Sunflower (*Helianthus annuus*)
- Sweet pea (*Lathyrus odoratus*)
- Nasturtium (*Tropaeolum majus*)
- Four o'clock (*Mirabilis jalapa*)
- Larkspur (*Delphinium Consolida*)
- Poppy (*Papaver* spp.)
- Love-in-a-mist (*Nigella damascena*)
- Snapdragon (*Antirrhinum majus*)

FLOWERS TO ALLOW TO SELF-SEED

- California poppy (*Eschscholzia californica*)
- Bachelor's button (*Centaurea cyanus*)
- Columbine (*Aquilegia* spp.)
- Alyssum (*Lobularia maritima*)
- Forget-me-not (*Myosotis sylvatica*)
- Cosmos (*Cosmos bipinnatus*)
- Foxglove (*Digitalis purpurea*)
- Black-eyed Susan (*Rudbeckia hirta*)
- Verbena (*Verbena bonariensis*)
- Hollyhock (*Alcea rosea*)
- Cleome (*Cleome hassleriana*)

MATURING IN THE GARDEN

Most flowers and herbs, and some vegetable seeds, germinate and grow better if they are allowed to mature and ripen right on the plant. When they are ready, simply collect them and store them in an envelope for next year. For this method, choose to harvest seeds on a dry day in the early afternoon when seeds are retaining the least amount of water.

For annual flowers, stop deadheading and allow the flowers to fade and the seeds to develop. Keep a close eye on them, because when the seeds have matured, they can disperse quickly.

Lettuce and cabbage seeds can be collected by placing a paper bag over the plant and tying it at the base when the plant begins to flower. When the seeds are ready, they will drop naturally into the bag.

Pea and bean seeds can be left until the pods are completely brown before harvesting. When collected, spread them out on a clean, dry surface and leave them to dry for a week. To check if they are dry enough for storage, bite one. If it is hard, it is ready to be packed up.

Flower seed pods such as nigella, poppy, coneflower, and sedum are beautiful enough to use in dried flower arrangements.

True heirloom tomatoes will grow true to seed, so pick the tastiest varieties to save.

Lemon cucumber (*Cucumis sativus* 'Lemon') seeds benefit from fermentation before drying to improve storage life. Cucamelon or Mexican Sour Gherkin (*Melothria scabra*) seeds can be dried directly without fermentation.

FERMENTING SEEDS

Some seeds need to be fermented to germinate properly. To induce fermentation, soak seeds in water for a few days until the pulp around them softens, then collect, dry, and store them.

Cucumber and melon seeds should be scooped from an overripe fruit, soaked in a mason jar half-filled with water, and left covered for 3 or 4 days. The best seeds will sink to the bottom. After drying on a paper towel, store them in a seed envelope.

Tomato seeds require a few more steps, but are worth the effort. Add just enough water to cover the seeds and surrounding pulp in a mason jar. Instead of sealing it, use a paper towel held in place with the jar ring. After a few days, mold will form on the surface, which signals that the seeds are ready to be strained and dried.

SCOOP OUT AND DRY

The scoop-out-and-dry method involves simply scooping seeds from inside vegetables and laying them out to dry.

Pumpkin and squash seeds are ready to harvest when the outer shell has hardened. Cut the vegetable in half, scoop out the seeds, rinse them, pat them dry, and spread them out until completely dry. Note that different varieties of squash and pumpkin can cross-pollinate, meaning the seeds you save might produce something unexpected. If you want to ensure a particular variety, purchase seeds from a trusted supplier.

Pepper seeds are ready when the peppers turn dark red, purple, or black. Slice them in half and, wearing gloves, remove the seeds. Spread them out on a paper towel away from direct sunlight and let them dry for 1 to 2 weeks before storing them in an airtight container.

Strawberry seeds are on the outside of the fruit, so you can simply crush the fruit on a paper towel and let it dry. When dry, fold up the paper and store it in an envelope. Because strawberry seeds are tiny, keeping them on the paper towel helps prevent loss; just ensure that the strawberry pulp is fully dry before storing to prevent mold growth.

THE CULTURAL SIGNIFICANCE OF SEED SAVING

The legalities surrounding seed saving for farmers and other gardeners impose on years of tradition. Before commercial seeds were available for purchase, generations of gardeners passed down seeds. It is a process that should still be honored today.

The World Trade Organization (WTO) governs many rules surrounding seed saving, and farmers in developing countries are increasingly affected by these regulations. Restricting access to seeds makes growing food inaccessible for many. As our population grows and biodiversity decreases, we need more people growing healthy, sustainable food. Swapping seeds and varieties with other gardeners and farmers also helps to increase biodiversity. Saving seeds holds cultural and environmental significance that must be considered before accepting that modern corporations control seed saving.

STORAGE AND EXPIRY DATES

To ensure longevity, store seeds in a cool, dark, and dry place. Always write the date you saved or stored them. When stored properly, a general rule is that seeds last for a year. However, most will last two to five years, and some can last for decades. Research your specific seed when saving, and add a best-before date when storing.

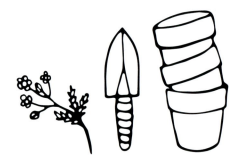

Poppy seed heads, like *Papaver cambricum* in front and *P. somniferum* can be shaken like salt and pepper on the garden to spread the seeds.

While purchasing seeds each year is a relatively economical method for growing a garden, seed saving is still an important practice. When you save seeds from your best-growing plants, you already know they can thrive in your garden. Year after year, your crop will get better and stronger as you continue to save only the best seeds. Seed saving is also a traditional process. For many, growing seeds passed down from older generations honors their history.

SEED SHARING PRACTICES OVER THE YEARS

When we buy seeds from a trusted supplier, we expect almost perfect germination and plants that grow true to type. Historically, seed sharing looked different. People would give a handful of seeds from a successful crop to a friend or neighbor, who could then plant them and hope for the same success. Variability and learning were more accepted, which added to the adventure! I love giving and receiving seeds because they are gifts that grow into months or years of connection and unexpected surprises.

Seed bombs made by mixing compost, wildflower seeds, clay, and flowers are a beautiful way to save and share seeds.

Starting Seeds

You truly can't get more wild and free in your garden than starting plants from seed. It brings back memories of growing beans or sunflowers in elementary school science class. It hasn't become more complicated since you graduated, but there are a few key things that will maximize your success.

Or are there?

Wind and animals have been dispersing seeds for much longer than we have been walking this Earth, so it's not really a human skill to master. That being said, there is a whole set of businesses out there that bank on highly successful germination rates and plants blooming or fruiting as expected.

Farms depend on seed-starting success to reduce costs and ensure crops are successful. Seed companies need quality to be exceptional to maintain their reputation. And growers don't want to waste time and materials on seeds that don't grow as expected. It's because of these needs that we, as home gardeners, think that seed starting is a specialized skill. Yet, we have volunteer seedlings all over our garden because some mammal pooped there.

While learning about the biology of seed starting can help us to increase success, germination, and reduce efforts and waste, there is no need for perfection in a home garden. More often than not we will have far more seeds and successful starts than we can plant and share. So give yourself some grace and just have fun.

Starting seeds is a great way to save money on full grown plants. Seeds are often accessible through seed swap events, seed libraries, and seed company donations.

SEED TYPES EXPLAINED

Heirloom Seeds

After World War II and into the 1970s, commercial vegetables dominated the market, making older varieties difficult to find. Heirloom seeds are those that have been cultivated for more than 50 years, passed down through generations, and remain true to the original plant. These seeds retain qualities such as beauty, flavor, yield, and resistance to pests, diseases, and weather. They are open-pollinated, meaning the parent plant's traits are preserved in the next generation.

Hybrid Seeds

Hybrid seeds result from cross-pollinating strong characteristics of different varieties to create new plants. They may have improved taste, disease resistance, or ease of growth. Hybridization allows for higher yields and uniformity, benefiting commercial growers. However, seeds saved from hybrid plants will not carry the same traits as the parent plant.

Open-Pollinated Seeds

All heirlooms are open-pollinated, but not all open-pollinated plants are heirlooms. Open pollination occurs naturally through insects, wind, birds, or human intervention. If a plant is pollinated by another of the same variety or through self-pollination, it remains an heirloom. If cross-pollination occurs with different varieties, it becomes a hybrid.

Organic Seeds

Organic seeds are grown and saved using certified organic methods. This does not mean that nonorganic seeds are treated with pesticides or herbicides, but rather that organic seeds come from farms with organic certification.

GMO Seeds

GMO seeds are created through biotechnology that merges DNA from different species. Currently, no GMO seeds are sold for home gardens; they are used exclusively for commercial crops. There is no need to search for non-GMO labeling on home garden seed packets.

Treated Seeds

Treated seeds are coated with an herbicide or pesticide to prevent fungal or insect damage. They are often brightly dyed and labeled as "treated." Many gardeners avoid treated seeds to prevent introducing chemicals into their gardens. Some coated seeds, like marigolds or lettuce, have a harmless coating to make handling easier. Always check seed packaging for details about treatments.

Bean seeds sprout quickly indoors allowing you to get a head start on the vegetable garden. Plant them when they have a few true leaves and you'll outsmart the pests who love to snack on tender seedlings.

HOW TO START PLANTS FROM SEED

Timing Is Important

Start by searching for your climate's last frost date online, in seed catalogs, or by asking a gardener. The last frost date indicates the date you can safely plant tender plants outside. Seed packets and growing instructions will list how many weeks before or after this date to sow specific seeds or transplant outdoors. Starting seeds too early makes them weak by transplant time, so stick to recommendations for best results.

Get the Light Right

Different seeds need different amounts of light during germination, which determines planting depth. Seeds needing lots of light get just a light soil covering, while those preferring darkness go deeper. Check seed packages for specific light requirements during germination. After seedlings start growing, they will generally need 12 to 16 hours of bright light daily.

Seeds won't need light until they emerge from the soil, but then they need strong sunlight most of the day to grow strong and sturdy. If sunlight's lacking, seedlings will get leggy (overly tall and floppy) as they reach for the light. Move them into brighter light or supplement the light with fluorescent lighting: grow lights made for seed starting or fluorescent shop lights both will work fine in the home garden setting.

Turn Up (or Down) the Temperature

Seeds have different soil temperature preferences to germinate. Some like it cool; others prefer warmth. Seed packets include soil temperature recommendations that professional growers follow precisely. For home gardening, simply separate seeds into those that need extra heat and those that don't. When starting indoors, we have to create these conditions ourselves.

Seeds that don't need heat can germinate fine in normal house temperature away from heat vents or direct sun. Heat-loving seeds do better on sunny windowsills, near heat sources, or on heat mats.

Humidity and Moisture Needs

Keep seeds hydrated by maintaining a moist (never soggy) growing medium. The medium should feel damp to touch but not waterlogged. Seeds thrive in humidity, so cover containers with clear plastic covers to create mini greenhouses.

Thinning the Weaker Seedlings

Seed instructions typically suggest planting two to three seeds per pot and keeping only the strongest. While you may hesitate to thin to one strong plant and try to separate and save them all, you could be doing more damage than good. Better to select the strongest and focus your energy on growing those well, than nursing all the seedlings back to health from division stress.

Hardening Off to Avoid Stress

If you are growing plants indoors, they need to be moved outside gradually to harden them off or acclimate them to outside conditions. Start by giving them a few hours a day near an open window or on a covered deck. Next, move trays outside, away from direct sun, starting with just 1 hour and gradually increasing to a full day. By the planting date, the plants will be hardy enough to be transplanted into the garden.

A small grow rack in a sunny window can be a successful way to start seeds, as long as you have supplemental light. Direct light is too hot for seed starting because it's magnified by the glass. Indirect light isn't bright enough on its own to signal growth. Also, the days are shorter early in the season, which also stunts growth. Grow lights provide a safe, bright light directly above the seedlings for the strongest starts and extend the light hours.

MATERIALS AND SUPPLIES FOR STARTING SEEDS

You can start seeds in almost anything that creates a mini-greenhouse. This is where your recycling bin comes in handy. These are the most basic seed-starting supplies you need:

Containers: Anything that holds soil, a seed, and drains water from the bottom works as a seedling pot. Old nursery pots, yogurt containers with holes poked in the bottom, toilet paper rolls, or newspapers rolled around a pot maker all do the job perfectly.

Seed Trays: These base trays hold your seedlings and allow bottom watering. Use seed-starting trays, repurposed plastic salad boxes, or any shallow container that can hold multiple seed containers and water.

Greenhouse Dome: Clear plastic domes from seed-starting kits hold humidity and warmth for germination, but you can also use plastic bags draped over pots, clear salad containers as mini greenhouses, or even a clear umbrella propped over your setup.

Soil: Use homemade seedling mix or store-bought seed-starting blend. As tempting as it can be, never use garden soil because it doesn't have the right structure and it exposes seedlings to bugs, bacteria, and fungi. Seedlings need light, well-draining soil that won't compact.

Plant Labels: Don't skip this step! You may think you will remember, but it's not worth the risk. Make labels from craft sticks, small branches, or cut-up plastic containers. Use permanent markers or grease pencils to ensure the labels don't fade.

PEAT-FREE SEED-STARTING RECIPE

This recipe is from my book *Garden Alchemy: 80 Recipes and Concoctions for Organic Fertilizers, Plant Elixirs, Potting Mixes, Pest Deterrents, and More.*

- 3 parts screened and sterilized compost
- 1 part coconut coir
- 1 part rice hulls (available inexpensively from homebrew supply shops, optional)
- 1 part perlite
- 1 part vermiculite

Grow Lights: Bright light from a greenhouse window works, but supplemental grow lights or fluorescent shop lights give you more control. Position lights 2 to 4 inches (5 to 10 cm) above seedlings and raise the lights as the plants grow to prevent leggy, weak plants.

Heat Mat: Gentle bottom heat speeds germination. Seedling heat mats work best, but you can use the top of your refrigerator or a heating pad (put a towel between the pad and tray because these can get hot and inconsistent).

Dividing perennials isn't just about getting free plants. Your perennials actually need to be divided to stay healthy. They clump and grow quickly, becoming crowded over time.

Dividing Herbaceous Perennials

There's a secret that professional gardeners and landscapers don't want you to know. When they're maintaining gardens, they routinely take divisions from plants from their client's gardens. This is not at all unethical, as the plants need to be divided to maintain their health. And these savvy gardeners have built this practice right into their business model.

I met one of these savvy landscapers when I found his backyard plant nursery posted in a Craigslist ad. He would pot up the divisions and sell them to gardeners, and his clients. This practice isn't uncommon, and it's brilliant. Perennials grow from divisions quickly into huge, bountiful transplants already proven successful in your climate. While perennials in 1-gallon (3.8 L) pots cost at least $10 (sometimes $40 or more), selling divisions for $5 to $20 is practically giving them away.

TIMING MATTERS

The best time to divide perennials is after they've finished blooming and before they go dormant. This gives plants time to recover without the stress of supporting flowers. Fall works perfectly for most perennials. The exceptions are irises, which prefer summer division after blooming, and fall bloomers, which should be divided the following spring. Fall division also gives roots more time to establish before the next growing season. You can divide plants in summer if needed, though it's harder for them to bounce back. They might look rough that growing season, but will likely recover by the following year.

Divide the plants when they look full, but before they become overcrowded. You'll know they're ready when a gap forms in center of the clump, the plants start flopping over, or they have simply spread too large for their space. Once crowded, their health drops and the centers can die back.

Work during cool parts of the day, in the shade, to protect divisions from additional stress.

STEPS TO DIVIDE PERENNIALS

1. Choose the right tool based on root density: a shovel for dense, compacted root balls and a garden fork for looser roots and soil. A fork causes less root damage, but it won't handle really dense, compacted root balls.

2. Work early in the morning and find a shady spot if you're digging in a sunny area. Move divisions to shade quickly to reduce stress on the plants. Lay a large tarp or blanket down to set the root ball on. This gives you a clean workspace to examine what you're working with.

3. Dig a perimeter 6 to 12 inches (15 to 30 cm) away from the plant's crown, going all the way around. Slide your shovel or fork under the root ball and push the handle toward the ground to pry the plant up. You might need to work from several sides to fully free it. Never grab stems and pull while roots are still attached to avoid breaking the stems. Keep digging around the perimeter and prying with your tool until the plant releases fully from the soil.

4. Shake off excess soil and examine the crown where roots and shoots meet. If there are smaller offsets on the mother plant, you can remove those for transplanting. For plants growing in larger clumps with multiple stems, use two garden forks to separate them. Place both forks back-to-back into the root ball where you want to divide, then pull them apart.

5. Some plants separate more easily than others. Hostas and daylilies often pull apart by hand, while ornamental grasses might require a saw to get through tough root systems.

6. Replant divisions right away. Prepare holes double the width of each plant and deep enough for the crown to sit at soil level. Backfill with soil, add well-rotted compost, and water thoroughly. Keep them well-watered for several weeks while they reestablish.

Propagation by Cuttings

Cuttings are one of gardening's most beautiful traditions: the simple act of sharing a piece of a plant with friends and neighbors. There's something magical about a gardener offering you a cutting when you admire a special plant in their garden. When you know how to nurture that cutting, you're not just adding a new plant to your collection; you're carrying forward a piece of someone else's garden story. You'll love seeing this generosity play out in plant-sharing groups, where gardeners start cuttings from their favorite houseplants, annuals, or prized specimens and offer them free to the community when they've rooted. While this extra step shows incredible thoughtfulness, don't feel you need to do the prep work, because growing roots from fresh cuttings is surprisingly simple. The truth is healthy plants produce so many potential cuttings that even dedicated propagators run out of space for them all.

GENERAL TIPS

There are two key factors that determine rooting success: high humidity and bright light. Cuttings need a humid environment so they don't dry out. Unlike seeds that don't need light to sprout, cuttings rely on photosynthesis to stay alive and grow new roots.

Rooting hormone isn't necessary, but it can increase success rates and speed up rooting. Rooting powder is available at garden centers; simply dip the stem in the powder. Willow branches contain natural rooting hormone, so if you have access to a willow, stick a branch in the water with your cuttings to encourage rooting.

Use the sterile seed-starting mix recipe posted on page 107.

Succulents root easily from small cuttings, but not all plants are as dependable. If you're running into issues, research propagation by cuttings for specific plants to see if there's an adjustment to timing or technique that might help.

Take cuttings when plants are not flowering. If it can't be avoided, just pinch off the flower buds.

WATER PROPAGATION

Water propagation is quick and decorative. Place the cutting in a clear glass container in a visible spot. It acts like a cut flower arrangement with a bonus: you can watch the roots grow. This method works well for houseplants and soft-stemmed herbs like mint and basil.

1. Cut just below a node (where leaves emerge from the stem), keeping three to four leaves on your cutting so it has enough energy to photosynthesize. Consider trimming large leaves in half to reduce water loss.

2. Submerge the cutting in water, making sure no leaves sit underwater. They'll rot and create bacteria problems. Place the container somewhere warm with plenty of light.

3

3. Refill water as needed to keep the nodes covered and replace it weekly or sooner if it gets cloudy.

4. Roots typically take 2 to 4 weeks to reach transplant size (about 1 inch [2.5 cm] long).

5. When ready, plant in premoistened soil, poking holes for each cutting or grouping several together for a fuller look. Water thoroughly and keep the soil consistently moist for the first 2 weeks to support root development.

4

STEM CUTTINGS

Stem cuttings work well for succulents, house-plants, herbs, and many perennials, shrubs, trees, and vines. They're planted directly into soil rather than water.

1. Cut 3 to 5 inches (8to 13 cm) from the stem tip just below a node, removing stems from the top third of the plant. Remove one or two lower leaves from the base and keep the top two or three. A few more is fine if they're small, but too many big leaves will pull energy away from root development.

2. Dip the cut end in rooting hormone, if you like.

3. Poke a hole in premoistened soil with your finger or a pencil, insert the cutting, and pat the soil gently around it. Because there are no roots for stability yet, you might need to prop it up. Cover with a clear plastic bag or green-house dome to help keep moisture in.

4. When you can tug gently and feel resistance, it's rooted. This usually takes 2 to 4 weeks for softwood cuttings and 6 to 12 weeks for hard-wood cuttings, depending on the plant species and conditions.

Lavender cuttings rooted in soil are a quick and easy way to get lots of full, bushy lavender plants.

SOFTWOOD VS. HARDWOOD CUTTINGS

Softwood cuttings come from fresh, green growth in spring or early summer. These stems are flexible and root quickly but need extra care to stay hydrated. Good examples include lavender, hydrangeas, and coleus. Softwood cuttings are great for many herbs, annuals, and fast-growing perennials.

Hardwood cuttings are taken in fall or winter from mature, woody stems. They root more slowly but are tougher and less prone to drying out. Common plants prop-agated this way include roses, grapevines, figs, and forsythia. Hardwood cuttings work well for woody shrubs and trees that go dormant in winter.

Angel Trumpet (*Brugmansia*) growing from cuttings in soil.

Succulents are so easy to propagate. A single cutting can quickly develop roots and grow into a new plant with minimal care.

LEAF CUTTINGS

Leaf cuttings work well for bushy, broadleaf plants because these can reproduce from a single leaf. Cut a single leaf with a small bit of stem attached. Dip the cut end in rooting hormone if desired and place it right side up in moist potting soil.

For some succulents, just the leaf is enough. Let the end develop a callus for one to two days, then set it on a bed of sterile soil. After two to three weeks, the leaves will shrivel and you'll notice roots. A few weeks later tiny leaves will emerge. The original leaf will eventually die off and decompose when you plant the new succulent in the soil.

Cuttings look great when grouped together in decorative pots.

PROPAGATING INDOOR PLANTS

Oh, the wonderful world of houseplants. What was once a quiet corner of horticulture has now bloomed into a full-blown cultural phenomenon. Proud self-identified plant parents have filled homes with fiddle leaf figs, pothos, and monsteras like outdoor gardeners scoop up perennials.

Whether you have been a lifetime houseplant lover or are just sprouting interest, this beautiful obsession comes with a new gardening community: one that loves uniqueness and cost savings, spurring a surge of interest in propagation.

This thrifty practice is no different than what we do outdoors (or can do outdoors, if we choose) but the community has helped this niche expand. It saves costs, it's fun, and it really couldn't be easier. When you see the prices on houseplants, it is almost comical to think that we ever purchased them potted.

There are four different methods for propagating houseplants: water propagation, stem cuttings, leaf cuttings, and division. For some plants, only one of the methods will work. For other plants, you can use multiple methods for propagating houseplants.

DOES TIMING MATTER?

Spring is wonderful time to propagate houseplants, as they too are waking up from a winter sleep, ready to produce some new growth. This means your new cuttings and plant babies are likely to grow quicker and easier; however you can propagate houseplants almost any time of the year.

HOUSEPLANTS TO ROOT IN WATER

- Pothos (*Epipremnum aureum*)
- Monstera (*Monstera deliciosa*)
- Begonia (*Begonia* spp.)
- Philodendron (*Philodendron* spp.)
- String of hearts (*Ceropegia woodii*)
- ZZ plant (*Zamioculcas zamiifolia*)
- Arrowhead vine (*Syngonium podophyllum*)
- Hoya (*Hoya* spp.)
- Peperomia (*Peperomia* spp.)
- Pilea (*Pilea* spp.)
- Prayer plant (*Maranta leuconeura*)

Exclusions: Lipstick plant (*Aeschynanthus* spp.), croton (*Codiaeum variegatum*), fiddle leaf fig (*Ficus lyrata*), and snake plant (*Sansevieria* spp.) can root in water, but do so slowly and less easily than others.

HOUSEPLANTS TO GROW FROM STEM CUTTINGS

- African violet (*Saintpaulia* spp.)
- Chinese evergreen (*Aglaonema* spp.)
- Coleus (*Plectranthus scutellarioides*)
- Ficus (*Ficus* spp.)
- Jade (*Crassula ovata*)
- Rex begonia (*Begonia rex*)
- Spider plant (*Chlorophytum comosum*)
- Wandering Jew (*Tradescantia zebrina*)
- Most other plants that root well in water also grow easily from stem cuttings.

HOUSEPLANTS TO GROW FROM LEAF CUTTINGS

- African violet (*Saintpaulia* spp.)
- Begonia (*Begonia* spp.)
- Jade (*Crassula ovata*)
- Peperomia (*Peperomia* spp.)
- Snake plant (*Dracaena trifasciata*)
- ZZ plant (*Zamioculcas zamiifolia*)
- Cactus (various species)—These are propagated from stem segments or pads rather than leaves, but the method is similar: Let the cutting dry until the cut end callouses, then plant in well-draining soil.
- Most succulents—While many are propagated from leaves, success varies by species and technique.

Neon pothos, *Epipremnum aureum* 'Neon', is as easy to propagate as it is to grow.

DIVISION PROPAGATION

Some houseplants produce pups (or offsets) that you can simply pull off with their roots intact and plant directly. Chinese money plant (*Pilea peperomioides*) is notorious for this. Overcrowded houseplants also make great division candidates if they have established root systems, especially plants with rhizomes, tubers, or multiple stems.

Remove the plant from its container and shake off excess soil. Gently pry apart sections, making sure each piece has good roots and leaves attached. If roots are tangled, use a sharp, clean knife to separate them.

Plant each section in moist potting soil, pat down firmly, and water thoroughly. Keep soil moist for the first few weeks while roots reestablish.

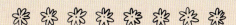

Pilea peperomioides pups are adorable tiny plants signifying good fortune. The divisions are so prolific and worthy of giving that they are also commonly known as a friendship plant.

✿ ✿ ✿ ✿ ✿ ✿ ✿ ✿
HOUSEPLANTS THAT GROW FROM DIVISIONS

- Alocasia (*Alocasia* spp.)
- Bird of paradise (*Strelitzia* spp.)
- Bromeliads (*Bromeliaceae*)
- Calathea (*Calathea* spp.)
- Chinese evergreen (*Aglaonema* spp.)
- Chinese money plant (*Pilea peperomioides*)
- Ferns (for example, *Nephrolepis exaltata*, *Adiantum* spp.)
- Oxalis (*Oxalis* spp.)
- Palm (clumping types, for example, *Chamaedorea* spp.)
- Peace lily (*Spathiphyllum* spp.)
- Peacock plant (*Goeppertia makoyana*)
- Prayer plant (*Maranta leuconeura*)
- Snake plant (*Dracaena trifasciata*)
- Spider plant (*Chlorophytum comosum*)
- ZZ plant (*Zamioculcas zamiifolia*)

4

WASTE LESS, GROW MORE: HOME-SCALE PLANT CONSERVATION

One of my favorite trees was a $15 Japanese maple, likely 'Bloodgood', that I picked up one fall at my local hardware store. It was crammed in a tiny 1-gallon (3.8 L) pot with just a few small branches and leaves. The stem, which would eventually become the trunk, had grown in an undulating curve, the result of constantly reaching for the light. It wasn't leaning to either side, just wavy, and interesting enough to adopt. I took the tree home and gave it a prominent spot in the garden: a large container in the center of the perennial bed. As it grew into a full-sized tree, that twisty trunk remained, giving it a strong yet playful character. Come fall, the leaves transformed into something almost supernatural: a red so vivid it seemed to burn from within. In the golden hour light, they didn't just glow; they blazed like stained glass windows lit by fire, leaving me breathless.

After growing the tree for fifteen years, I sadly had to leave it behind in my last move. The pot it was in was too large and fragile to safely move, and the maple was clearly very happy in place. I may have had to leave that tree behind, but I will certainly never forget its beauty. That little maple's journey from clearance rack to garden centerpiece shows us something bigger: The most rewarding gardens often grow from the unexpected. The rainbow of plants available to us is an excess of what we could ever need, and perhaps through reclaiming or recycling plants, we are doing so much more than getting a discount.

These days we tend to place more value on things that cost more. In fashion, for example, we often buy items on sale simply because they're cheap, even if they don't fit well or suit us. Those clothes then sit unworn in our closets until they end up as waste. Plants on sale can be bought just as impulsively, but the outcome is different. Even if forgotten, a plant will break down into compost instead of heading to the landfill. In other words, a clearance sweater only loses value, where a discounted plant is just beginning its story. It could provide a season's worth of food, attract pollinators, or grow into the centerpiece of the garden. This chapter is about working with plants as partners, not products. We will see them in a new light as we rewild our yards, rescue nursery orphans, keep favorite plants alive through the winter, and embrace chaos.

~~~~~~

Opposite: Sneezeweed in the Ambleside Pollinator Garden, West Vancouver.

Collecting and Propagating Native Plants

All the propagation methods we've covered work beautifully with native plants, and there's something especially grounding about growing species that belong in your landscape. The benefits are substantial: They're lower maintenance with built-in resilience, they support local wildlife, they improve soil health, and they have an overall positive impact on biodiversity and our environment. That said, native plant propagation requires deeper education because not every plant you find in the wild is actually a beneficial native species.

The common use of the word "weeds" is really about location: Any plant growing where we don't want it, like in our garden beds and lawns, is often considered a weed. But this location-based labeling doesn't tell us whether a plant is actually beneficial or harmful to our local ecosystem. What matters more is understanding whether these uninvited plants are friends or foes. Native plants are indigenous species that evolved here over thousands of years and have established relationships with local soil and wildlife. Invasive plants are often introduced by humans and disrupt ecosystems by out-competing natives. Learning to identify which is which helps us make better decisions about what to encourage, what to remove, and what's worth propagating in our gardens. Ironically, acquiring wild native plants can be complicated.

THE TROUBLE WITH COLLECTING WILD NATIVE PLANTS

Collecting seeds, cuttings, or divisions from wild plants in nature or public spaces might seem like the perfect way to get plants for free and support native species, but there are ethical and legal factors to consider. Regulations vary widely around the world depending on land ownership, conservation status, and local laws. Some areas require permits, while others prohibit collection entirely. Always get permission when needed, and never take from rare or threatened species. Collect only small amounts, spread out over time and space, and leave enough behind to support healthy ecosystems.

Native species like this Canada Goldenrod (*Solidago canadensis*) create beautiful, long-lasting, resilient garden spaces that rival the most manicured landscape design.

Creeping buttercup (*Ranunculus repens*) takes over the garden quickly and smothers nearby plants. Even though many people have fond childhood memories of putting the bloom to your chin to determine if you like butter, this plant is not a food source to native species and should be removed. And who were we kidding? Everyone likes butter.

UNDERSTANDING INVASIVE SPECIES

Invasive plants are typically introduced species that proliferate and take over spaces. They threaten natural ecosystems by out-competing local species and can change soil and water conditions while disrupting natural habitats. Removing invasives is important but often difficult because they're so prolific at reproducing themselves. When you're propagating plants, make sure you can positively identify natives versus invasives by double-checking with invasive species databases online.

FORAGING FOR FOOD VS. FORAGING FOR PLANTS

If I can forage for wild plants to eat, why can't I forage for plant divisions and seeds? Collecting plant materials for propagation differs from foraging for wild plants as food. Food foraging typically harvests naturally regenerating parts like fruits or leaves, or collecting mushrooms while leaving spores behind. Taking cuttings, seeds, or divisions can affect a plant's ability to reproduce and sustain its population if done improperly.

ACCESSING NATIVE PLANTS FOR PROPAGATION

As gardeners wanting to propagate natives, we must either start from seed or find specialized nurseries offering starts for division or cutting material. However, most mainstream nurseries carry limited native species and sometimes include invasives in their offerings. Seed variety is greater than potted plant options, and many natives actually prefer being started from seed because they can develop stronger root systems adapted to your specific soil conditions. Education remains key even when shopping at trusted suppliers.

How to Source Native Plants for Propagation

Seed swaps from local native plant groups offer free or low-cost seeds from local varieties, perfect for starting your propagation journey from scratch.

Community restoration projects sometimes allow volunteers to take surplus plants after planting events, giving you established material for division.

Wild spaces on your property likely contain native plants you can divide and relocate using the division method in chapter 3 (page 108).

Friends or neighbors with private properties might share plants for propagation. Use the same division and cutting techniques covered in chapter 3.

Your own land's seed bank can be accessed by removing turf grass to allow dormant native seeds to emerge. Seeds can remain viable in soil for 5, 10, even 100 years, until conditions support growth. Creating open garden spaces and being informed and intentional with weeding allows you to identify which plants are native versus invasive.

PROPAGATION TIPS FOR NATIVE PLANTS

Native plants often respond differently to propagation than typical houseplants or garden varieties.

Seed Starting: Many cool-climate natives need cold stratification (winter simulation) before germinating. Place seeds in damp sand in the refrigerator for 30 to 90 days before planting.

Division: Native clumping plants like wild ginger or native grasses divide best in early spring or fall, when they're not actively growing.

Cuttings: Take cuttings from native shrubs in late summer when growth has hardened off. Use rooting hormone and be patient, because some natives can root more slowly than cultivated varieties.

Water Propagation: Some natives like willow or elderberry root easily in water, while others prefer going straight into soil.

WILD BEAUTY AT RISK

Some of the most enchanting native plants, like lady's slipper orchids (*Cypripedium* spp.) and blue cohosh (*Caulophyllum thalictroides*), are also some of the most threatened. These woodland perennials are prized for their ornamental (lady's slipper) or medicinal (blue cohosh) value in shady gardens, but they are slow to grow and often depend on specific soil fungi to survive. Wild specimens rarely survive transplanting, and over-collection has caused steep declines in natural populations. To protect these fragile beauties, always source them from reputable nurseries that grow them from seed or lab-propagated starts.

Flats of annuals can be heavily discounted or donated mid-summer.

Rescue Plants: Acquiring Heavily Discounted or Free Plants

There are many places you can get plants for free (or almost free) if you know what to look for. Community plant sales usually offer divisions of perennials or extra seedlings. End-of-season clearance racks at nurseries and garden centers are another good source. There are plenty of plants available if you're willing to do a little digging.

JUST ASK

When planning the décor for a large summer garden party, I called a local pop-up garden center and asked if they would have plants available for donation when their locations shut down. They were thrilled at the request and invited me to pick any leftover plants I wished for the party. When I arrived at the location, they had so many huge mixed annual planters that I had to make multiple trips. I used the gorgeous planters as decoration for my garden party. After the party was over, all of these plants and containers went to my guests so they could enjoy their blooms for the remainder of the summer, and keep the decorative pots to plant in future years.

GARDEN CENTERS

Garden centers often have racks of plants that didn't sell or annuals that are dying back. Seasonal stock changes mean these plants can be heavily discounted, donated, or sometimes just left for disposal. Hardware stores and big-box garden centers usually have a clearance section with plants in rough shape. They might look like they're on their last legs, but if the roots are still healthy, they're usually fine once you cut them back and give them a bit of care. Hardware and grocery stores often set up a seasonal expansion of the regular garden center in a section of the parking lot during the busy garden shopping months. These pop-ups shut down in midsummer, so call and ask if you can partake in any end-of-season donations they may have.

LANDSCAPING AND CONSTRUCTION

Connecting with landscaping companies and checking construction sites can lead to great plant salvage opportunities. Sadly, mature trees and shrubs often get dumped during renovations, and if you can rescue and relocate them, you'll save money while giving these plants a second life. Timing and preparation are important factors to successful transplanting, so do what you can to advocate for proper removal. Collection during the dormant season has the best success for transplanting, but you may not have much choice.

Removing trees and shrubs is a big job, so the landscaper or construction company might be planning the chop the tree down rather than excavate it. Homeowners often offer these trees and plants up as U-dig specials, meaning if you can dig it up, you are welcome to take it. If you have the tools and skills to do the job yourself, then you can likely get some beautiful mature specimens for your garden by trading your labor. If you don't have the skills or equipment for removal, you can still offer to give them a home, and in many cases, landscapers and contractors will work with you, to a point. You will still have to do the transplanting and transport, so roll up your sleeves, get some help, and get ready for the job.

How to Transplant a Large Tree

Bigger trees require serious planning because you need substantial root balls, and that means thinking through logistics like equipment (like dollies, trucks, maybe professional movers), access routes, and potential obstacles like walls or power lines. While it may not be possible, if you have advance notice you can root prune months in advance. This builds a dense root mass that will survive the move. It's the gold standard for big tree transplants.

TRANSPLANT DURING DORMANCY

In most cases, dormancy is between late fall after leaf drop and early spring before bud break. That window is the best time to move a tree to minimize shock. Water the tree well in advance.

GET A BIG ENOUGH ROOT BALL

The American Standard for Nursery Stock (ANSI) Z60.1 provides detailed specifications for root ball sizes based on trunk caliper: 10 to 12 inches (25 to 30 cm) of root ball diameter per 1 inch (2.5 cm) of trunk caliper (measured 6 inches [15 cm] above ground) and a depth 60 to 75 percent of that diameter. For example, a 4-inch (10 cm) trunk needs a 40 to 48-inch (102 to 122 cm) diameter root ball that's 24 to 36 inches (61 to 91 cm) deep to ensure transplant success.

Dig a trench at the desired width and depth, then dig under the root ball to loosen it and remove it from the soil.

KEEP THE ROOT BALL INTACT AND MOIST

Wrap the root ball in burlap and don't let the soil dry out. Move it the same day if possible.

REPLANT IMMEDIATELY AT THE SAME DEPTH

Dig a hole that is twice the diameter in width but match the depth. To avoid planting the tree too deep, you will match the original soil line.

WATER THOROUGHLY AND CONSISTENTLY AFTER PLANTING

Deep watering weekly for at least the first full season (or longer) is critical for reestablishment.

Even if you do all of these things correctly, there is no guarantee that a transplant will take. Many factors such as age, species, and overall health can cause the transplant to fail, even if you follow all of the steps. If the tree is particularly special or valuable, reach out to an expert with tree-moving experience and equipment. Contractors who specialize in transplanting large trees have the tools (like tree spades or cranes) and know-how to get this right. Or just go for it! Your attempt at transplanting could be a wild success or a valuable learning experience. Either way, it's a better fate for the tree than being chopped up for firewood.

Transplanting large trees means you'll need to dig up a very large root ball.

How to Transplant a Shrub

Shrubs are more manageable for DIY moves, though they can still have surprisingly extensive root systems. A friend with a shovel can usually handle smaller ones, but larger shrubs can have impressive root systems and be just as large as trees.

Root ball size for shrubs is less exact than for trees and varies by species, age, and health. As a rough guideline, use 12 to 18 inches (30 to 46 cm) per 1 foot (30 cm) of shrub width to ensure enough roots stay intact.

When transplanting, dig a hole twice as wide as the root ball and the same depth, backfill with soil, and water deeply to help everything settle in.

When transplanting shrubs, be sure to plant them to the same depth they were in their previous site.

WHAT TO LOOK FOR WHEN GETTING DISCOUNTED OR RESCUED PLANTS

First and foremost, check that the plant is healthy. That means no pests, no disease, and nothing that's going to cause problems in your garden later. A plant might be wilting or dying back, but that doesn't always mean there's something wrong. Perennials, for example, often die back in their dormant season, and the same goes for deciduous trees and shrubs. It's important to know the difference between dormancy and decline.

Start by identifying what kind of plant it is. If there's no label, you're taking a risk. It could be invasive, toxic, or just something you don't want in your garden. Try to get a botanical name if possible, and if you don't know the plant, do a quick search to learn its growing requirements. You don't want to bring home a shade plant when your whole garden's full sun, or something that grows 10 feet (3 m) tall when you can only plant in a tidy border.

If it's an annual, faded flowers are fine, but stems and leaves need to be healthy. Flowers can be deadheaded to encourage more blooming. Look for buds. If the leaves or stems are dying, it's not going to bounce back.

Perennials, on the other hand, can be a great deal if you're familiar with the plant and you know it's healthy. Even if it looks like nothing more than sticks and soil, go for it. Garden centers have a heck of a time selling perennials that have stopped blooming because most folks pick up the pretty plants when they shop. In fall, you can usually score some great free or cheap perennials, and it's a great time to plant them. They will not look like much in the garden this season, but they will have time to settle in and make a big comeback in spring.

Before taking home discounted or rescued plants, be sure the roots are still relatively healthy and the plant is free of pests, even if the stems and leaves are wilted.

With trees and shrubs, when they're not leafed out, it's harder to tell if they're healthy, so pay close attention to the soil and root conditions. You can tell if the branches are dormant or dead by feeling the wood. Cool wood has some water flowing still, but wood that is air temperature is likely dead. Cut a branch to look for green (alive) or brown (dead) wood to be sure.

Do a Thorough Health Check

When the top of the plant checks out, gently pull it out of the pot and check the roots. You're looking for firm, healthy roots that smell like fresh soil. If they're mushy, smelly, rotting, or the plant is root-bound and choking itself, that's a red flag. It's best to stick with healthy plants to start.

Also take a look at the soil. Problems aren't always obvious, but try to make sure there are no weeds or hitchhikers in there such as invasive seeds, insects, or fungus gnats.

Better Safe Than Sorry

When you've decided to bring a plant home, especially from a plant sale or rescue situation, strip off the soil. Wash the roots and replant it in fresh soil. That way, if there's anything nasty in the original mix like fire ants, soil-borne disease, or fungal spores, you're not introducing it to your garden. You can rinse off the top growth, too, to remove anything that might be hiding on the stems or leaves. There's always a bit of risk with bringing home outside plants, but if you do your due diligence, chances are good you'll end up with a healthy, happy addition to your garden.

The roots of this rainbow chard are not only healthy, but also quite pretty. The root colors match the stems so they are easy to separate.

CHOOSE WISELY
Take It Home
- A perennial that has finished blooming or gone dormant
- Annuals with unopened buds
- Healthy roots and soil, even if the foliage looks rough

Leave It Behind
- Annuals that have finished blooming or died back
- Rootbound or diseased roots
- Annuals already flowering and fruiting in tiny pots (for example, a 4-inch [10 cm] tomato plant with fruit, unless it's a dwarf variety)
- Leggy, weak seedlings had a bad start and will struggle to thrive

AVOID THE FOUR Ds
Avoid anything that shows signs of the four Ds: dead, dying, diseased, or damaged (beyond repair). Skip plants with visible pests. Don't take the risk. Disease and pests are dealbreakers.

Overwintering Tender Plants and Annuals

Sometimes we get attached to our plants. I have yet to meet a gardener who didn't have at least one special relationship with a beloved plant and go the extra mile to tend to it. In cold climates, it's common to see neighbors wrapping tropical trees in burlap and lights, moving their prized Meyer lemon tree into the greenhouse, or taking cuttings of their begonia collection for next year's hanging baskets.

This extra effort pays off in multiple ways. By over-wintering your favorite plants, you save money, preserve special varieties, and get a head start on next year's garden. Plus, those overwintered cuttings and divisions become perfect offerings for plant swaps and community exchanges come spring. Don't worry if they look a bit scraggly by spring. You've done the hard work, and these survivors will bounce back beautifully once they're back in their element.

The level of winter protection your plants need depends on both the species and your climate zone. Hardy perennials might survive outdoors with minimal care, while tender perennials and tropicals need to come inside in northern climates. Annual flowers and vegetables worth saving can be propagated through cuttings, especially if they're expensive or hard to find. Bulbs, tubers, and corms like dahlias, cannas, and caladiums need to be dug up and stored in cooler climates.

Where you overwinter your plants matters just as much as how you do it. Indoor grow lights work best for herbs and small flowering plants that stay active year-round. A greenhouse is the dream for overwintering, but if you don't have one, a cool basement or garage with temperatures between 45°F to 55°F (7°C to 13°C) is ideal for dormant plants like bulbs, trees, or perennials. Semihardy plants might need a protected outdoor area with shelter from wind and extreme cold, while some plants require an indoor growing station with consistent light and warmth.

Cuttings of these tender plants can be taken at the end of the season and overwintered in a greenhouse.

Snow may look threatening to plants, but it is an excellent insulator protecting the soil and roots below. Some tender leaves may get damaged, but they will fall off and be replaced in the spring. It's what's going on below the surface that is most important.

OVERWINTERING IN THE GARDEN

The easiest way to overwinter plants is to leave them in the garden. Hardy and semihardy plants can stay in the garden with a few steps to prepare and insulate them.

Leave flower heads in the garden so that the seeds feed wildlife. Leaving plant material to decompose naturally is part of the natural cycle, but remove anything that's going to cause harm to the plant like weeds, disease, or pests.

Weed and add a layer of mulch to insulate the soil and prevent the ground from freezing.

Plants that are more tender can benefit from being wrapped with burlap, cardboard boxes, horticultural fleece, or even a string of Christmas lights to generate a little warmth.

MOVE CONTAINER PLANTS

Tender container plants should be moved before the first hard frost of the season. Simply moving them under a bench, deck, or the eaves near the house where the microclimate is warmer could save the plants and pots wear and tear. For more protection, move them to a greenhouse, garage, or basement. Check thoroughly for pests like aphids, spider mites, or whiteflies (look under leaves and at stem joints), rinse the foliage, and even consider repotting with fresh soil if pests have been visible.

Over the winter, reduce watering frequency to every two to four weeks. A garage or basement that gets a couple hours of light per day when plants are dormant should be fine.

For tender trees like citrus or palms, gradually acclimate them to indoor conditions before the first frost. Start reducing watering but maintain humidity, and when you move them, place them in the brightest possible location and slowly prepare them for dormancy. Greenhouses are great for this because you can maintain both humidity and temperature while overwintering plants.

TAKE CUTTINGS OF PRIZED ANNUALS

Taking cuttings works perfectly for plants like coleus, impatiens, geraniums, succulents, and many herbs. Follow the instructions for "Propagation by Cuttings" (page 110) in the previous chapter.

DIG UP AND STORE THE WHOLE PLANT

Bulbs and Tubers

1. To overwinter tender summer-flowering bulbs, tubers, corms, and rhizomes, wait until the first light frost causes the foliage to die back or the leaves to drop. Then carefully dig up the plant, taking care not to damage the bulbs, tubers, or roots.

2. Shake off loose soil and trim away any dead or damaged foliage.

3. Let the plant parts cure in a dry, well-ventilated spot out of direct sunlight for three to seven days. This allows cuts and bruises to dry and helps prevent rot during storage.

4. When cured, place them in breathable containers such as cardboard boxes, paper bags, mesh sacks, or wooden crates. Surround each one with dry peat moss, vermiculite, or sawdust to absorb excess moisture. Avoid using plastic, which can trap humidity and lead to decay.

5. Store them in a cool, dark location between 45°F and 50°F (7°C and 10°C). Check periodically throughout winter for any signs of shriveling or rot, and remove any affected pieces right away.

6. Label each variety before storing so you'll know what's what when it's time to replant in spring after the danger of frost has passed.

Dig up dahlia tubers when the flowers die back of after the first frost.

Perennials, Trees, and Shrubs

For tender dormant perennials, trees, and shrubs, you can dig them up, pot them, and overwinter them like container plants.

1. Use a sharp spade to dig around the drip line, several inches from the stem, and lift the plant with the root ball intact. Trim any broken roots.

2. Pot in a container slightly larger than the root ball with good drainage. Add fresh potting mix, place the plant in the center, and fill around the roots.

3. Water thoroughly and let it rest in shade outdoors for a few days before moving indoors. Water only when the soil is dry a few inches down.

4. In spring, gradually reintroduce the plant to light and warmth before planting it back outdoors.

Group together tender plants and seasonal pots to store over winter.

CARING FOR OVERWINTERED PLANTS

Most overwintering plants need significantly less water in winter. Let soil dry between waterings and never let plants sit in standing water.

Dormant plants need minimal light, while active growers need bright locations.

Most overwintering plants prefer cooler temperatures from 55°F to 65°F (13°C to 18°C), except for tropicals.

Check regularly for pests like aphids and spider mites, which love the warm, dry indoor air and can multiply rapidly.

RETURNING THE PLANTS TO THE GARDEN

When it's time to return plants to the garden, patience is key. Don't rush this part. Wait until all danger of frost has passed, then take your time hardening off plants over one to two weeks. Your patience will pay off. Start with a few hours in dappled shade, gradually increase exposure to sun and wind, and bring plants in at night initially. Keep soil consistently moist during transition, hold off on fertilizing until plants show active growth, and monitor for stress, providing temporary shade if needed.

While the plant may be hardy, the container it is growing in may not. This bonsai Japanese maple tree doesn't have enough root coverage to overwinter. It's best in the greenhouse until spring.

THE ULTIMATE OPTION

A greenhouse is the ultimate season extender. It protects tender plants in winter, allows for earlier seed starting and later harvests, and it can be a showstopping design feature in your garden.

Joan Fedoruk's one-of-a-kind greenhouse is made from reclaimed stained glass windows, wood, and houses a stunning crystal chandelier.

Embracing Chaos Planting

I've been a longtime fan of chaos planting, which means scattering seeds and allowing nature to do the work of naturalizing the space. I learned this technique over twenty years ago from a good friend who lived across the street from me. She didn't want to buy all the plants for her large garden space because she rented her home. Instead, she purchased a few packets of perennial flower seeds and scattered them on the soil. Over time, the garden showed which seeds were hardy enough to survive in her space and grew abundantly. My friend would dig up and divide overgrown perennials or move them to more appropriate locations throughout the growing seasons. Before long, the garden looked like it had been landscaped by a pro. And it had. Mother Nature did most of the work.

Chaos planting embraces natural, informal arrangements of plants rather than neat rows or particular patterns. It takes away the rigidity of planting instructions and allows for more wildness. It follows the way plants grow in the wild, encouraging biodiversity and resilience by mixing species and allowing the strongest to thrive. Starting a garden from chaos means scattering seeds broadly across an area without spacing or rows, allowing plants to grow where they land and self-manage over time. Embrace the chaos with these tips to get started.

Group plants with similar needs. Plants that like full sun and well-draining soil can be grouped together, ensuring they get scattered in the right areas.

Opt for native species. These seeds are much more likely to germinate and thrive on their own because they're adapted to your area's sun, water, temperature, humidity, and soil conditions.

Consider local regulations. Things like plant height bylaws or strict HOA rules can limit what you plant and how you plant them.

Stomp your seeds. After you scatter your seeds, walk around and press them into the soil. This helps prevent seeds from blowing away.

Water your seeds. After scattering, give the area a good watering to kickstart germination.

Aftercare. You can choose to leave it completely wild, or you can go in and thin seedlings, water plants, or add compost and fertilizer.

Try chaos gardening with herbs and vegetable seeds. Scatter seeds like basil, lettuce, or carrots into your already established vegetable garden and watch these veggies fill in the extra spaces.

replacing lawn with a wildflower meadow

My wildflower lawn has turned my house into the talk of the town. What was once a drab, uneven, and neglected lawn has turned into an urban meadow that is not only stunning but also incredibly low maintenance and eco-friendly.

When I first considered removing my lawn, I thought about what would actually thrive in the space. I decided on a wildflower lawn alternative seed blend from a well-respected local seed company, knowing it would have the best chance in our climate. What I loved about the blend was how it promised waves of color throughout the season: early bloomers giving way to midsummer flowers, then late-season blooms, with annuals, biennials, and perennials all mixed together.

Because I was working with existing lawn, I didn't bother removing all the grass. The fescues in my seed mix would complement whatever stayed. I spread 3 inches (8 cm) of topsoil mix over everything, then tried something unconventional with the seeding. Instead of following the packet timing exactly, I sowed three times: a few weeks early, on schedule, and a few weeks late. This gave me better coverage and filled in gaps naturally.

What resulted was the most stunning and low-maintenance front yard I could imagine. Because each time I sowed the seeds before it rained, I watered zero times. I then built a dry river through the lawn as a pathway and as a result, I mowed zero times. Drought tolerant, no mow, beautiful, and regenerative: After you try a wildflower lawn, you will never go back.

MATERIALS:

There are only two materials you need for this project: seeds and soil. You may have the soil prepared already, but in this project I topped my existing turf grass with lawn soil mix (20 percent sand mixed into compost) and a wildflower seed blend from a local supplier.

My blend was the Wildflower Alternative Lawn Mix from West Coast Seeds containing:

- Baby blue eyes (*Nemophila menziesii*)
- California poppy (*Eschscholzia californica*)
- Creeping daisy (*Chrysanthemum paludosum*)
- Dwarf California poppy (*Eschscholzia caespitosa*)
- Five spot (*Nemophila maculate*)
- Hard fescue (*Festuca trachyphylla*)
- Johnny jump-up (*Viola cornuta*)
- Sheep fescue (*Festuca ovina*)
- Sweet Alyssum (*Lobularia maritima*)
- White Dutch clover (*Trifolium repens*)
- Wild thyme (*Thymus pulegioides*)
- Yellow daisy (*Chrysanthemum multicaule*)

SELECTING AND PREPARING

Select a seed blend suited to your growing conditions and desired plant mix. Herb, perennial, butterfly, shade, and drought-tolerant blends are widely available; look for those identified as lawn alternative. Local suppliers offer seeds adapted to your climate, improving success rates. Quality blends provide succession blooming throughout the season, with early flowers transitioning to midseason and late bloomers through a mix of annuals, biennials, and perennials.

If converting lawn, you can leave existing grass in place, especially if your blend includes complementary grasses like fescue. Prepare the area by weeding, then spread 3 inches (8 cm) of lawn topsoil mix evenly across the surface. Rake the soil level before sowing.

SOWING

1. Order 15 to 20 percent more seeds than the area requires to fill patchy areas after germination.

2. Sow seeds three times rather than once: several weeks before the recommended date, on the recommended date, and several weeks after. This extends germination periods and improves coverage.

3. For the first sowing, use a straight rake to work seeds into the top 1 to 2 inches (2.5 to 5 cm) of soil.

4. Subsequent sowings can be scattered directly between existing seedlings.

MAINTENANCE

Keep seeds consistently moist during germination according to packet instructions. Drought-tolerant mixes may require no additional watering after establishment if timing coincides with natural rainfall patterns.

5

BUILDING BELONGING
THROUGH PLANTS AND PEOPLE

Traveling Cuba's roads, you'll be struck by the vibrant beauty of the many vintage American cars from the 1940s and 1950s. Since the U.S. Embargo in 1962 made parts and vehicles nearly impossible to obtain, Cubans became masters of ingenuity, welding Soviet truck parts into these classic cars and making new parts from scrap metal. While I recognize the risk of romanticizing resilience from an outsider's perspective, I am genuinely moved by the creative solutions people use to repair and restore rather than discard and replace.

Along those same roads you will hear and see music and dancing as Cubans gather on their front stoops to share food and socialize. This connection was deeply woven into the culture long before economic challenges. But 60 years of scarcity has made sharing and community the true wealth, beyond material possessions. These long-standing economic difficulties have created real hardships that I don't want to minimize. Yet these same challenges have cultivated remarkable innovation and strong community bonds.

By contrast, I notice how many of my Canadian neighbors nestle inside their homes watching television as I walk through my neighborhood each evening. On public transportation, people spend time on their phones instead of people-watching, chatting, or enjoying the scenery. No wonder we're facing rising loneliness. Perhaps our access to material abundance has created a different kind of constraint, with screens becoming tethers that keep us isolated from genuine connection.

I'm not alone in noticing this shift. Generations are growing up yearning for reconnection with our Earth, our land, and each other. The community that was once part of rural or farm life is being sought again. There's a resurgence in off-grid living, homesteading, and people embracing the idea of moving away from larger, busier urban cultures. But the move to less populous areas doesn't equal isolation from others. Instead, these communities build stronger connections with surrounding neighbors to thrive.

I felt this acutely when I moved into my new home as a single parent. With a dog, cat, house, and school-aged child to care for, I lacked the time and skills to repair everything that needed fixing. Plus, many projects required physical strength, stamina, or multiple sets of hands that I simply didn't have alone. I found myself hiring labor and digging myself deeply into debt for the privilege of assistance.

Thankfully, I had a village to call on for many tasks. Moving a dresser from one bedroom to another, hanging artwork, assembling garden beds, and picking up pavers from my Buy Nothing group were just some of the ways my friends pitched in, saving me the $50/hour price tag of hired help. Their generosity saved my nervous system from overwhelm and my spirit from loneliness.

Community is invaluable, but in this day and age, you need to actively build it. Yes, you can find and join existing communities, but it's just as important to learn how to invite and create the environment for connection yourself. To have a village, you have to become a villager. Once you're contributing, you become part of that connected web.

In this chapter, you will see numerous ways that you can build community through the sharing economy and gardening. Start small with getting a garden BFF and trading plant care work, hosting a plant potluck, or lending tools. Revive old school practices like work parties, skill sharing, and group purchasing. Then dive in to explore some big ideas like land sharing and collectively owned buildings.

Strong communities don't just happen. They come about through participation, generosity, and consistency. If you want connection, it means showing up for others without keeping score to create the trust, safety, and belonging that we all crave. In a culture where individuals are becoming increasingly isolated and independent, it takes intentional time and effort to begin building those connections. This is where it begins.

SIX EASY WAYS TO BE A VILLAGER

1. Share your harvest. Give someone a handful of freshly picked tomatoes or a basket of lettuce from the garden.
2. Mow your neighbor's hellstrip (the skinny piece of land between your front sidewalk and the curb) or boulevard when you do yours.
3. Give a passing stranger a jar of cut flowers from your garden.
4. Offer to lend a tool to a co-worker you know they need.
5. Invite the members of your neighborhood group to join a local egg farm CSA delivery.
6. Invite a workout buddy over for a cup of mint tea harvested from the garden.

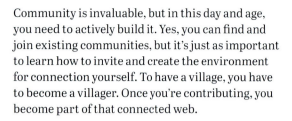

We are too quick to discard treasures that have fallen out of fashion. These pieces take on a new life in the garden.

These two neighbors share a common space between their houses and use it as a gathering space. Chairs set on both sides of the winding pathway that leads into their individual back gardens invite conversation and connection.

Meet Your Garden BFFs: Garden Buddy System

While plants have consistent care needs, you'll inevitably have a time when you need someone to take over the task: a Garden Buddy. They act as a plant sitter when you go on vacation or foster your plants while you move houses. A Garden Buddy can be a huge help when you are feeling unwell, recovering from surgery, or just having a tough week.

Maybe you have a neighbor with a little lawn space right next to yours. Instead of watching them lug a lawnmower out to that small patch every week, why not mow their lawn when you're doing yours? They may bring you tea in thanks, or offer to prune your side of the hedge. At very least, you and your neighbor will both get the emotional benefit from kindness. And who knows? It could be the beginning of becoming Garden Buddies. The true value comes from building the type of connection that goes deeper than temporary help.

Thankfully, you do not need to be monogamous with a Garden Buddy. Feel free to expand your circle to multiple neighbors who have different needs. If you have the tools and skills to prune hedges, you could offer to help neighbors who hire a service for hedge trimming a few times a year. Everyone will save some money and you could negotiate weekly weeding, tomato harvesting, or winter snow shoveling in return. The goodwill connects you with your neighbors and gives you backup when you need it. I guarantee you'll find bouquets from their blooming lilac tree on your doorstep, or baskets of vegetables when their harvest is overwhelming. You'll have the comfort of knowing you're part of a larger support system.

HELPER'S HIGH

Helping others gives us a release of happy brain chemicals like dopamine, serotonin, and oxytocin, known as the "helper's high." Simply allowing someone to show you kindness is a gift to them.

PLANT FOSTERING

For prize plants needing special care, arrange a plant foster program in your neighborhood for when you can't tend to them or when a plant's needs exceed your capabilities. Maybe one of your garden friends has deeper skills to rehabilitate an ailing plant and teach you along the way. Post plants needing care in your network and request volunteers to take them for fostering.

Please feel
welcome
to sit...or enjoy
a game.

A Garden for Gathering

As you approach Karen Reed's heritage home in East Vancouver, you will be invited to play a game of Jenga at the table on her boulevard. It marks the type of community feeling that she has created in her intergenerational community home. The house features six bedrooms, three bathrooms, and many rooms to gather in, including the garden. For over fifteen years, the members of this house have changed but the concept has remained the same: Connection with others gives us a sense of belonging.

Grow Together with Shared Greenhouse Space

Many urban gardeners dream of having a greenhouse to start their seeds or overwinter tender plants, but can't spare the space to house one. Instead of duplicating resources, community members can share greenhouse space or rent a bench in a neighbor's greenhouse. Extending the idea beyond the physical structure to share the supplies and tools inside allows people to garden together and share knowledge as well. These shared spaces can be structured in various ways.

CO-OWNERSHIP

A group jointly owns the greenhouse and shares the space equally. This collaborative model allows community members to divide costs and maintenance responsibilities. The community would meet to discuss which tools and supplies will be communal versus individually owned.

SPACE RENTAL

The greenhouse owner rents space to others in exchange for work contributions, tools, harvest shares, or financial compensation. The owner manages the building while renters use the space.

INCLUDE TOOLS AND SUPPLIES

Stock the greenhouse with the basics, like heating and cooling systems, watering equipment, hoses, sprayers, watering cans, waste buckets, compost bins, plant markers, gardening tools, soil containers, potting mix, and nursery pots. This way, greenhouse membership is turnkey for all who participate.

Shared outbuildings like greenhouses and sheds offer the community functional space without the constraints of individual ownership, especially in urban areas where space is at a premium.

POST POLICIES FOR EVERYONE

Creating clear usage rules is essential: plants should be labeled, respect for others' property maintained, and specific notes about plant care or tool usage made available. Implementing a "clean as you go" policy ensures the space remains tidy for all users.

Pop-Up Gardens: Growing on Shared Land

Not everyone has access to a backyard, and even those who do might find themselves drawn to the collaborative energy of shared gardening spaces. Gardening alongside others offers knowledge exchange that's impossible when working alone: learning which varieties thrive in your specific climate, discovering pest solutions that actually work, or simply having someone pick your tomatoes while you're traveling. There are multiple ways to access land, ranging from very organized to more grassroots approaches.

COMMUNITY GARDENS

Community gardens are the most structured way to get your hands dirty alongside other gardeners. They come to be when interested citizens approach the landowner (the city, province, state, or other entity) and ask to create a garden space. They can emerge in empty lots, commercial properties, or temporarily underdeveloped building lots. The group looks for funding to build the space and then leases individual plots to community members with annual renewals. This approach is highly organized, requires substantial work, and beautifies spaces while giving you a built-in community of people to learn from.

STRATHCONA COMMUNITY GARDENS

The Strathcona Community Gardens occupy 3.34 acres (1.35 hectares) of city land on the Vancouver Eastside unceded traditional territories of the xʷməθkʷəy̓əm (Musqueam), Sḵwx̱wú7mesh (Squamish), and səlilwətaɬ (Tsleil-Waututh) Nations. Community volunteers restored the land and built 110 individual plots on a former dump site in 1986. The space now is home to a solar-powered eco pavilion, an herb garden, a greenhouse, a Buddha pond, a children's garden, an apiary, a mushroom log garden, and one of the largest heritage orchards in the province. It is a truly beautiful and productive place that provides opportunity and connection for gardeners.

Collaborative housing is often framed by a collaborative garden like this perennial flower garden at a multi-family dwelling.

Rows of edible flowers grow between leafy greens at a sharing farm.

CO-HOUSING AND CO-OP HOUSING

Co-housing is an intentional living community where people purchase smaller homes connected to communal spaces like shared kitchens, clubhouses, playgrounds, and gardens or farms. These spaces are shared by all community members.

Co-ops differ from co-housing as communities where people collectively own shares of a property. They also have shared spaces such as rec rooms, playgrounds, gardens, and other communal areas that allow community members to get involved beyond their individual living spaces.

Both of these collective living community structures tend to have shared garden spaces.

SHARING FARMS

The next approach is sharing farms, which are similar to community gardens, but instead of individual plots, people come together to work on a farm collectively. Everyone who contributes to the farm work becomes part of the community supported agriculture (CSA).

In this model, members work on one larger space together and then participate in the harvest, whether it's food, flowers, or other products. For example, members might all work on a flower farm and share in the bounty.

Pollinator pathway gardens allow for beneficial insects to travel through neighborhoods.

This neighbor's pink Japanese snowbell tree (*Styrax japonicus*) attracts enough bees to pollinate everyone's vegetable gardens.

GREENWAY COMMUNITY PROJECTS

Moving toward less organized, more grassroots approaches, there are greenway community projects. These are urban projects that beautify public spaces in neighborhoods. This might be tending a roundabout in the middle of a residential area, building a medicine wheel garden, or creating a food forest in a public park for all citizens to enjoy.

NEIGHBORS' GARDENS

Another approach involves landowners sharing their property with someone willing to do the labor of tending a garden, with both parties sharing the harvest. Similarly, neighbors might help each other out. Perhaps one neighbor isn't using their yard, so another neighbor takes over maintaining it.

RENTALS

Renting is not an unusual means of sharing garden space. Either you rent land in a garden, or rent farmland to pursue farming or gardening activities elsewhere. Find these by searching for "land sharing" in classified ads, on social media, or in community spaces like community centers, shops, or libraries in the area you want to rent land.

host a plant potluck

"There are little pots of plants for everybody to take when they leave," announced my friend LoriAnn Bird at her book launch. Friends and family attended the celebration at Salish Friendship Centre to celebrate her beautiful book, *Revered Roots*, and in true LoriAnn style, she gave everyone a gift from her garden to take home. Inside each 4-inch (10 cm) recycled nursery container were four plants: a sprig of sweetgrass, a wild strawberry, a raspberry cane, and a yarrow division. It reminded me that sharing plants is such an easy and inexpensive thing to do, but also a powerful way to build community connections.

A potluck allows us to gather together while avoiding placing uneven burden on the host. It takes the pressure off so the host also can enjoy the party and spend time with loved ones. Taking this idea out to the garden makes it even more fun: time with gardeners and you get to go home with new plants. What's not to love?

Organize your party by theme or embrace the true potluck style: simply allow everyone to bring whatever they have. When you have no expectations about what they'll bring, allowing the "luck" part of potluck to unfold naturally, it creates its own magical experience. This approach frees us from the structure of needing to be in control and helps to balance those who *have* with those who *need*. The generosity of

My favorite aspect of attending a permaculture design is the daily potluck lunch. This sharing and connection time gave everyone an opportunity to discuss the concepts in a deeper way and learn about each other's lives. Instead of sitting alone with individual lunches, we came together, sharing little pieces of ourselves through food.

gardeners means people will bring what's available to them and share that abundance with those who most need it.

Hosting a plant potluck requires minimal effort, just an open heart and space to gather. It gives us the chance to open our homes to community while growing something in our garden that continues to connect us to our loved ones and friends. A plant from our garden can be divided many times, shared, and watched as it sprouts up around neighborhoods and communities. When we visit those houses and see the "mother plant," we know we have a piece of it at home. It connects us to the land and to the people who tend it.

PICK A DATE AND THEME
Choose a time that fits the season: spring for seedlings, summer for cuttings, or fall for divided perennials. You can set a theme or keep it open potluck style where guests bring whatever they have.

CREATE AN INCLUSIVE INVITATION
Welcome everyone, no matter how much or little they bring. Emphasize that the spirit of the swap is generosity, and that bringing something is not a requirement. It's those who have the least to share that have the most need.

CHOOSE AN INDOOR OR OUTDOOR SETTING
In winter, host an indoor swap where people bring houseplant cuttings or plants they no longer want. In warmer months, hold an outdoor gathering where guests can display plants in labeled, recycled nursery pots.

SET SIMPLE SWAP RULES
Use an easy system like "bring one, take one" or "bring five, take five" to keep things organized, while setting up a secondary "free for all" table that anyone can stock up from. Encourage gardeners who need more plants to stick around to the end and take home whatever is left over.

LABEL PLANTS CLEARLY
Ask guests to label plants with botanical names and basic light and care instructions to make it easy for others to choose plants that will thrive in their gardens or homes.

host a soil party

Organizing a soil party with your neighbors offers a smart way to reduce the overall cost of acquiring soil in spring while avoiding the expense and plastic waste of buying bagged soil in small containers. Coordinate with neighbors to order soil and amendments in bulk and have them delivered to a common space, perhaps in front of your home, where everyone can collect their share using buckets to create their own mixes.

As the organizer, you might structure neighbors' monetary contributions to cover both the soil costs and compensation for your organizational efforts, trading your labor for benefit rather than paying out of pocket. Another approach is to host a "potting soil potluck" where neighbors gather and each brings a specific ingredient for the overall soil mix: you provide the compost, a neighbor brings coconut coir, another brings perlite, someone else contributes vermiculite, and another brings nutrients. Mix everything together in a large wheelbarrow and divide it into containers for everyone to take home.

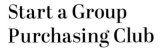

Start a Group Purchasing Club

When purchases are necessary, organizing group buys can dramatically reduce costs. As an organizer, you might cover the cost of your materials or earn a few extra bucks by charging participants a small fee. The structure is straightforward: one person organizes a buying community around a specific topic, approaches suppliers, and creates a sign-up spreadsheet. Retail prices become wholesale rates through economies of scale.

Group buys work best for items that benefit from bulk purchasing: Think soil, compost, and mulch from landscape supply yards. As individuals, we pay premium prices for bags or buckets, but a delivered truckload shared among community members saves big. Seeds also offer excellent value when purchased in quantity, as do seed-starting supplies, plants, and bare-root trees.

Other ideal candidates include garden fabric, shade cloth, row covers, drip irrigation systems, stakes, tomato cages, trellis materials, rain barrels, and compost bins.

HOW TO ORGANIZE A GROUP PURCHASING CLUB

Establish Your Platform: Create a communication hub using a social media group, email list, or messaging app. This will serve as your central coordination point for all group activities.

Build Your Membership: Recruit members through social media posts, email groups, community boards, and word of mouth. Make the sign-up process simple and clearly communicate the benefits of joining. Allow members to share the group with others easily.

Identify Group Interests: Survey members about their product needs and encourage suggestions for potential group buy items.

Source Reliable Suppliers: Research reputable, eco-conscious suppliers that align with your group's values. Request wholesale quotes and note minimum order requirements.

Manage Orders and Payments: Always collect orders and payments upfront before placing wholesale orders. This protects both the organizer and ensures commitment from members. Use digital payment platforms for easier tracking.

Structure Your Pricing: Arrange wholesale pricing with suppliers, then present options to the group. Add a small administrative fee to cover the organizer's time and effort, or offer free products to the organizer as compensation.

Assign Coordination Roles: Avoid burnout by designating a rotating coordinator role to help with communication, order reminders, and pickup logistics.

Set Up Distribution: Establish convenient central pickup locations, ideally with a community member who has adequate storage space. The distribution point host should receive some benefit for their service, as this is a big job. Develop a clear system for labeling orders and scheduling pickup times.

Start Small and Scale: Begin with one or two items to test your process and gather feedback from members.

Tips for Success

- Set clear expectations about timing and delivery.
- Keep detailed records of orders and payments in accounting software or a thorough spreadsheet.
- Build relationships with reliable suppliers.
- Regularly seek feedback to improve the project.
- Focus on items that offer significant savings when bought in bulk.

neighborhood tool-lending program

A tool-lending program is a community resource with the power to reduce a great deal of waste. Most neighborhoods have hundreds of houses with hundreds of sheds containing hundreds of rarely used hedge trimmers, lawn edgers, and loppers. By sharing, we cut wasteful overconsumption and make these tools more accessible to beginners and folks with limited incomes.

Beyond the practical benefits, these programs also build trust and collaboration. Lending tools gives us a chance to offer something useful to our neighbors while extending responsibility. This act of trust can elevate community members and bring us together.

HOW TO ORGANIZE A TOOL-LENDING PROGRAM

Storage and Location: Choose a central, easily accessible location for the shed, ideally somewhere within walking distance for most participants. A front or side yard, community garden, school, church property, or neighborhood center are good choices. The shed itself should be weatherproof and secure. A lockable door is ideal, with access through a shared combination lock.

Build Inventory: Begin with commonly used tools, and gradually expand through community donations, grants, and hardware store partnerships. Post in local groups that you're collecting tools for a community sharing initiative and encourage the program members to donate their seldom-used tools.

Organize the Shed: Use labeled shelving, pegboards, or bins to separate types of tools. Store heavier items low to the ground and protect delicate tools from being buried or dropped.

Set Up a Checkout System: Hang a clipboard with a log sheet, a small whiteboard, or the QR code to a digital form at the entrance. Each tool can be labeled with a number or bar code to manage inventory. The easier it is to check out tools, the more likely people will do so responsibly.

Assign Maintenance Duties: To maintain the shed and tools, create a rotating volunteer system. Schedule regular community inspection and cleaning days, assigning maintenance roles to members. Encourage users to report any broken or dull tools without fear of blame. Clearly mark a "repair bin" for ease of returning the tools for service.

Determine Lending Periods and Logistics: Set basic borrowing guidelines, perhaps starting with seven day periods and easy renewal options for longer projects.

BUILDING TRUST

If you're committed to the community-building aspect, consider implementing a trust-based system with flexible lending times. Because everything is donated to the community, there's room for adaptability in lending periods. If someone needs a tool for 6 months, let them keep it. Organizers can follow up when others are waiting for the same item or consider acquiring additional popular tools. It can be surprising how easily members self-regulate when fewer restrictions are placed on their behavior.

BASIC TOOLS THAT EVERY GARDENER NEEDS

These tools are helpful to have in the tool-lending program, although regular gardeners will likely need these on site at their garden. The tool-lending program mandate could collect and distribute these to members of the community who need them, but not add them to regular inventory.

- Hand trowel (with depth measurements)
- *Hori Hori* knife (soil knife)
- Hand pruners (secateurs)
- Garden gloves
- Watering can or hose and watering nozzle
- Hand rake or cultivator
- Small spade or transplanting shovel
- Garden scissors or snips
- Knee pad or kneeler
- Bucket or trug

TOOL-LENDING PROGRAM TOOL LIST

- Wheelbarrow or garden cart
- Large shovels
- Garden forks
- Loppers and pole pruners
- Hedge trimmers
- Soil auger or bulb planter
- Post hole digger
- Leaf blower
- Power washer
- Chainsaw
- Seed spreader
- Soil sifter or screen
- Orchard ladder or tripod ladder
- Tree-planting auger
- Stump grinder
- Flame weeder
- Grow lights (for seed starting)
- High-quality pruning saw
- Sod cutter
- Concrete mixer

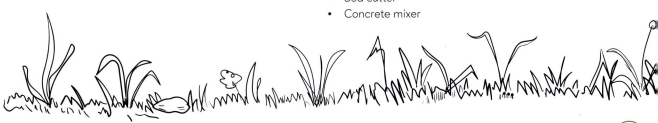

present skill-sharing workshops

I learned to grow potatoes back in my community garden days. A fellow gardener, an elder who spoke no English, generously shared her knowledge through demonstration. After giving me seed potatoes, she invited me to her plot and showed me the large trench she had dug for planting. Each time I visited the garden afterward, I noticed how she continuously mounded soil up to the emerging leaves. What began as a deep trench gradually transformed into a tall mound throughout the growing season. By harvest time, we could dig down nearly 4 feet (1.22 m) to uncover an abundance of potatoes.

Skill-sharing workshops build community resilience by passing down practical, time-tested knowledge about successful gardening methods and Earth stewardship. This approach is remarkably easy to implement because communities already contain vast stores of diverse knowledge within their members. We often spend considerable money attending large conferences and educational events, but overlook the wealth of knowledge that exists within our own communities.

Skill-sharing workshops celebrate community wisdom, honor diverse cultural traditions, and build connections through shared learning while strengthening our collective gardening knowledge and neighborhood bonds.

Inviting a few friends over to plant mini cut flower gardens is a fun reason to gather. I hosted a workshop on how to plant summer blooming cut flower bulbs and top the containers with spring annuals that the bulbs will grow through in summer.

HOW TO HOST
SKILL-SHARING WORKSHOPS

A workshop series where individuals volunteer to teach specific skills to members of the community could be hosted at individual's homes, similar to a book club. Individuals can sign up to share their expertise each month, gathering around a potluck meal, harvest sharing, or similar event, with one person leading a knowledge-sharing session about their gardening practices.

Knowledge-sharing topics needn't be complex or extensive. Simple techniques and practical demonstrations are welcomed by members. Including a "show and tell" component enhances these skill-sharing workshops. As participants arrive, each person brings something to share such as a unique plant, a garden photo, vegetables or flowers, a hand-crafted item, a successful recipe, a useful technique, or an innovative tool. This informal sharing creates a casual atmosphere to learn from each other.

SEASONAL PRESERVING WORKSHOPS

Preserving workshops help garden groups make the most of their harvest while cutting down on food waste. Plus, they capture summer flavors and revive skills from the past. Learning the techniques for canning, fermenting, drying, and freezing reduces dependence on imported products and makes the most of homegrown harvests.

These workshops work best from late summer into fall when harvests are plentiful. Start them in midsummer so folks can prepare, then continue through fall to build those skills. At season's end, host a harvest party where everyone brings something they've canned, fermented, dried, or frozen for a community swap.

For these workshops, you need access to kitchen equipment. Depending on group size, you could meet at a member's home with a large kitchen or set up a portable kitchen outdoors. If there's enough neighborhood interest, consider looking for space with a suitable kitchen at a housing co-op, church, or community center.

GARDEN TOOL REPAIR CLINICS

Tool clinics reduce waste and promote sustainability while building the skills of time gone by. In the modern day, tools are too often discarded when they simply need maintenance or repair. By learning to maintain and restore, gardeners gain a deeper understanding about how the tools work and develop greater appreciation for their equipment.

Activities could include sharpening, handle replacement, rust removal, and basic care. Structure the clinic as a drop-in where members bring their broken tools to volunteer experts for repair. The experts should come equipped with spare parts, necessary tools, proper safety gear, and practical knowledge. If your garden group lacks such expertise, reach out to a local hardware store and ask if they would host your group. Most would welcome community members learning repair skills; it builds goodwill and they can sell replacement parts. Many stores might even offer educational programs themselves.

Schedule drop-ins in early spring before growing season starts and again in the fall for end-of-season maintenance.

CHILDREN'S GARDEN EDUCATION PROGRAMS

Kids' programs instill environmental values and gardening love from an early age. These programs give children eco-literacy while young, building healthy habits and nature connections many adults are missing.

Activities could include planting, composting, pollinator education, butterfly raising, or creating garden art. Offer these workshops as summer programs or after-school activities for garden-loving parents wanting to share childcare responsibilities. A couple of parents can volunteer as teachers to give the other parents some free time for errands or rest while knowing their children are engaged in something worthwhile. Teachers can rotate, keeping the children engaged while giving all parents occasional breaks.

Get crafty with paint and flowers to beautify recycled containers for a kid-friendly garden project.

When you teach a child to garden and they fall in love with plants, they'll grow up to protect the Earth.

create a neighborhood garden work party collective

One of my favorite experiences from my community garden was our monthly work parties. These gatherings transformed what might seem like solitary chores into collaborative social events where we got loads of work done in short periods. Hosting neighborhood work parties offers a wonderful way to connect with neighbors while supporting community members who could use a hand with larger garden projects.

HOW TO HOST A NEIGHBORHOOD WORK PARTY

Gather interested neighbors and establish a regular monthly date for working on each other's projects. Start with an initial meeting to discuss the skills, tools, and supplies each person can contribute. Outline potential projects that could be completed in a workday, such as repairing fences, assembling sheds, weeding garden beds, installing (small) patios, building arbors, or creating herb spirals.

Schedule a work party per month for 6 to 10 months of the year (6 months if you're limited by seasonal weather, or up to 10 if you live where outdoor gardening continues year-round). Match the number of households who participate to the number of annual work parties so each family hosts one work party in the year. Encourage consistent participation by allowing absences for emergencies only. If someone regularly misses work parties, their project might need to be bumped from the schedule.

The project owner prepares all materials and develops a plan for their work party. Group members can help refine these plans leading up the scheduled work party. Plan for two monthly gatherings: a planning session (combined with a potluck) where participants discuss upcoming projects, arrange schedules, coordinate materials, evaluate needed skills, and plan work party details; followed by the actual work party.

Similar to a permablitz, the homeowner hosting a work party typically doesn't participate in the physical labor. Instead, they serve as the day's supervisor by providing food, ensuring everyone has necessary tools and information, clarifying project details, and coordinating the overall effort. Though they won't be doing hands-on building or planting, their role coordinating, feeding, and supporting participants is crucial to the work party's success.

PERMABLITZ

A permablitz, similar to an old-fashioned barn raising, is a community project where a group gets together to build a project based on a permaculture design. For example: planting a food forest, building a water catchment system, or building a chicken coop.

traveling suitcase program

A traveling suitcase program is a sharing initiative featuring a suitcase, box, or backpack filled with useful garden items passed from person to person within the community. It's about fostering connections among gardeners while contributing to the sharing economy. It's a way to share things you don't need and discover items that might benefit your garden.

The items included should be nonperishable and small enough to fit in a suitcase.

ITEMS TO INCLUDE

- Small hand tools like pruners, trowels, or cultivators
- Extra seed trays or plant markers
- Seed packets (likely the primary component)
- Extra bulbs or divided plants
- Gardening gloves or kneeling pads
- Garden aprons or sun hats you're not using

You can also include handmade items from your garden:

- Homemade healing salves or herbal teas
- Seed bombs
- Shelf-stable preserves like jam
- Garden photos made into cards
- Eco-printed cards or handmade paper
- Pressed flowers or leaves

5. Include a nonperishable garden-related gift for the next person.
6. Label everything clearly so people understand what the items are.
7. Pack up the suitcase and deliver it to the next person on the list.
8. Ensure the journal and core items remain in the suitcase.
9. Keep the suitcase clean, dry, and well cared for (don't leave it out in the rain!).

Items should be:
- In good, usable condition
- Small enough to fit inside the suitcase
- Nonperishable
- Not overly heavy (no bricks!)

Do not include:
- Expired products
- Seeds older than two years
- Diseased plants or materials
- Invasive species

This system creates a continuous cycle of giving and receiving while building community connections through shared gardening knowledge and resources.

HOW IT WORKS

Start with creating a sign-up sheet to gather participants. You could recruit from a neighborhood group, book club, local social media group, or post a sign-up sheet at your local library or community center.

MATERIALS:
- A sturdy carry-on sized suitcase
- A few starter tools
- Some seed packets or seed bombs
- A couple of small gifts
- Gardening books
- A beautiful blank book to serve as the garden journal

RULES:
Include these in the first pages of the garden journal.

1. Keep the suitcase for one week.
2. Feel free to take anything you need from the suitcase.
3. Replace what you take with items for the next gardener.
4. Add your entry to the journal including information about who you are, a gardening story, tip, sketch, or poem.

A key component is a garden journal. Each participant writes a note to the next gardener with:

- A piece of gardening wisdom or tip
- A short story about their garden
- A sketch of something in their garden
- A meaningful poem or quote
- Photos, pressed leaves/flowers, or drawings

A garden journal creates a living document of community knowledge that grows with each participant who adds their personal touch.

conclusion

As we've gone through the wild and free journey together, we've unlearned some things. We've loosened the grip on a way of living that kept us isolated, overworked, and overwhelmed. We've questioned the idea that comfort or happiness can be bought, and instead started to recognize that giving up some things makes room for more of ourselves.

We've gone so far down this path, but this was never how we were meant to live: sitting alone in boxes, overwhelmed by our to-do lists, surrounded by too much stuff, and completely disconnected from each other. We're meant to live in groups; to share parenting, chores, tools, and the harvest. We're meant to laugh with our neighbors, borrow a cup of sugar, and pass the time together.

That's a wild and free life.

When I talk about cost-saving as the main concept for this book, I don't just mean the money saved by spending less or finding free things. Yes, that, but also the deeper cost to our mental health, our physical well-being, and our attachment to community. The high cost of anxiety, overwhelm, and disconnection from nature shows up in our cells. Warm hugs, engaging conversations, and daily closeness with the people around us are the things we give up, the price we pay, for busyness.

Here, in the wild & free way of living, there is hope. We can pause. We can breathe. We can ask ourselves what we really want, and find that most of it can't be ordered online or built into an app.

It isn't about making do. It's about having enough. Not because we're forced to, but because we no longer want to feed a system that trades joy for convenience and wastes resources that still have value. When we choose secondhand, salvaged, shared, and repurposed materials, it feels good to use what we already have. And it brings us closer to one another. Those exchanges don't happen through a screen or a big-box store; they happen with our neighbors, our friends, our family, and our communities.

The things that matter are the ones we grow, share, and tend together. You've already begun. Every choice you've made along this path, every saved seed, every shared harvest, every moment spent with hands in the soil, has brought you closer. You're not separate from this. You're part of it now.

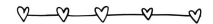

Let the wild in.
Be free.
Grow.

about the author

After many years in the corporate world as a marketing director, Stephanie Rose's life changed overnight in 2006 when a sudden illness confined her to bed for almost two years. What could have been a tragedy instead transformed her life completely, as she discovered gardening as a way to heal and her new life became rooted in purpose.

Starting in her urban East Vancouver yard, Stephanie's passion for gardening grew alongside her healing. She became a Vancouver Master Gardener in 2010 and dedicated the next ten years to building children's gardens while earning certifications as a permaculture designer, herbalist, and natural skincare formulator. With a deep passion for bringing gardening to everyone as a tool for healing and regeneration, she focuses her work on community building, accessibility, and making gardening simple and approachable for all.

Through her international speaking and writing, Stephanie advocates gardening as a tool for community building and environmental restoration alongside personal growth. She is the best-selling, award-winning author of thirteen books. Her previous titles include: *The Regenerative Garden: 80 Practical Projects for Creating a Self-Sustaining Garden Ecosystem* (Cool Springs Press, 2022), *Big Book of Botanical Crafts* (Better Day Books, 2022), *Garden Alchemy: 80 Recipes and Concoctions for Organic Fertilizers, Plant Elixirs, Potting Mixes, Pest Deterrents, and More* (Cool Springs Press, 2022), and *Garden Made: A Year of Seasonal Projects to Beautify Your Garden and Your Life* (Roost Books, 2016), which was a gold medal winner in the Independent Publisher's Book Awards.

In 2009, Stephanie created her website, Garden Therapy®, www.gardentherapy.ca, as a way to create an online community dedicated to making gardening accessible to everyone, regardless of space, budget, or ability. She has reached millions of people around the world with the message of "living a better life through plants" and has devoted herself to the restorative connection between plants and people. She lives in a small urban home in East Vancouver with her kiddo, dog, cat, and 500 worms, and continues to cultivate a garden where healing, joy, and connection grow side by side.

acknowledgments

It is with deep gratitude to the many members of my community of friends, coworkers, gardeners, and neighbors, who have been part of my village, that I am able to write this book.

I'm grateful to live on the east side of Vancouver, on the unceded land of the xʷməθkʷəy̓əm (Musqueam), Sḵwx̱wú7mesh (Squamish), and səlilwətaɬ (Tsleil-Waututh) Nations. The Musqueam and Tsleil-Waututh speak hən̓q̓əmin̓əm̓, while the Squamish speak Sḵwx̱wú7mesh sníchim. Both languages belong to the Coast Salish branch of the Salish Language family, which dates back many millennia.

My neighborhood of East Vancouver is special, where front gardens are creative, open, and welcoming spaces for connection and community. The gardeners here visit with each other, share plants, and exchange stories of how we can become better stewards.

I deeply appreciate the gardeners I've met through the Vancouver Master Gardeners, and other local garden groups. I've been inspired by many local garden tours including the East Van Garden Tour and Arts in the Garden in North Vancouver from North Van Arts, which is supported by Vancouver's North Shore Tourism Association. These events gave me the opportunity to privately visit some of the most beautiful gardens to photograph for this book.

I want to acknowledge the organizations that do such great work to educate and support community building: Keep It Green Recycling, The Neighbourhood Small Grants program, City Farmer, Yarrow Ecovillage, Buy Nothing, ChipDrop, West Coast Seeds, Flowerbulb.eu, and Figaro's Garden.

Thank you to the gardeners who opened their doors to share some of their beautiful projects: Delphia Johnstone, Joan Fedoruk, Laurel Walker, Wendy, Monica and Brad, John White, Inga, Susan Koelink, Susan Lee, Sue Bath, Karen Reed, and the Strathcona Community Gardens.

To the team at Quarto, who treats authors as partners and supports my ideas (even though they are different from any of the others out there) helping to bring them to life so beautifully. My brilliant editor, Jessica Walliser, is patient, professional, and so knowledgeable, that I know I'm in good hands. Steve Roth has provided both top-shelf book marketing and friendship. Thank you also to Kerri, Heather, Gabrielle, Cindy, Tim, Lorraine, and the team involved in the making of this wild and free book.

To my wonderful friends who helped me when I needed strength and heavy lifting: Jaydene and Adam, Miriam and Chris, Kimmy and Gerald, Lindsay and Antonio, Gerry, Eugenio, Allison, Jamie, Neil, Eimmy, and Kathrin Beckmann of K. Beckmann Gardens. I'm grateful for your generous willingness to help.

To my favorite budding gardener, Asher, who shares his love for nature as much as I do. You've been gardening with me since before you were born, and have become so strong and capable. You moved rocks, named the plants, and protect the bees. Keep growing, kiddo, and maybe one day you'll be taller than the sunflowers!

You are all my community and my village, and I wouldn't want to do this wild and free life without you.

index

Karen Reed, 143
Sue Bath, 71
Susan Lee, 59
invasive plants, 120, 121, 122

J

jade (*Crassula ovata*), 116
Japanese maple, 119
Johnny jump-up (*Viola cornuta*), 136
Johnstone, Bob, 62
Johnstone, Delphia, 62–63
journals. *See* garden journals

K

Keep it Green Recycling Reuse, 43
kids' programs, 158

L

lady's slipper orchids (*Cypripedium* spp.), 122
land care societies, 48
land rental, 147
landscaping companies, 123
larkspur (*Delphinium consolida*), 98
leaf cuttings, 114
learning spaces
    botanical gardens, 48
    colleges, 49
    community centers, 49
    libraries, 49
    universities, 49
leaves, 82
Lee, Susan, 59
lettuce, seed collection from, 97
libraries, 49
light
    assessment, 27
    cuttings and, 110
    Deep Shade, 27
    Full Sun, 27
    garden map classifications, 34
    Part Shade, 27
    Part Sun, 27
    Shade, 27
    shadow patterns, 34
    sun path, 34
love-in-a-mist (*Nigella damascena*), 98
lumber. *See* reclaimed wood

M

maps. *See* garden maps
marigold (*Tagetes* spp.), 98
Master Gardener programs, 48
materials. *See* equipment
melons, seed fermentation from, 99
metal outdoor furniture, 67
methyl bromide (MB), 78
microclimate assessment, 31
monstera (*Monstera deliciosa*), 116
municipal programs, 51

N

nasturtium (*Tropaeolum majus*), 98
native plants
    accessing for propagation, 122
    collecting, 120
    propagating, 120
    sourcing, 122
native plant societies, 53
natural reproduction, 96
natural stone, 85
neighborhood apps and networks, 46
neighbors' gardens, 147
neuroscience, of garden journals, 25

O

open-pollinated seeds, 103
organic seeds, 103
outdoor furniture
    foraging, 66
    indoor furniture repurposed as, 69
    restoring, 67
outdoor solar chandelier, 64–65
overwintering
    container plants, 129
    cuttings and, 130
    in garden, 129
    overwintered plant care, 131
    returning to garden, 131
oxalis (*Oxalis* spp.), 117

P

pallet wood, 78, 86
palm (*Chamaedorea* spp.), 117
Part Shade plants, 27
Part Sun plants, 27
pathways, 83

patio pavers, 85
patios, 83
peace lily (*Spathiphyllum* spp.), 117
peacock plant (*Goeppertia makoyana*), 117
peas, seed collection from, 97
peperomia (*Peperomia* spp.), 116
peppers, seed collection from, 99
perennial division, 108–109
permablitzes, 159
Permaculture Design Certificate (PDC), 48
permaculture groups, 48
permaculture zones
    flexibility of, 35
    introduction to, 35
    Zone 0 (Home Zone), 36
    Zone 1 (Garden Zone), 36
    Zone 2 (Food Forest), 38
    Zone 3 (Farm Zone), 38
    Zone 4 (Woodland Zone), 39
    Zone 5 (Wild Forest Zone), 39
philodendron (*Philodendron* spp.), 116
pilea (*Pilea* spp.), 116
planting
    chaos planting, 132
    permablitz, 159
    seed starts, 104, 105
plants. *See also individual plants; seeds*
    assessment, 29
    community groups, 46
    Deep Shade, 27
    fostering, 140
    Full Sun, 27
    genetically modified organisms (GMOs), 97
    indoor plants, 115
    invasive plants, 121
    labels for, 106
    native plant sourcing, 122
    natural reproduction, 96
    Part Shade, 27
    Part Sun, 27
    perennial division, 108–109
    plant potlucks, 148–149
    propagation by cuttings, 110–114
    Shade, 27
    threatened species, 122
    weeds, 120

shrubs
  rescuing, 123
  transplanting, 125
skills-for-skills barter, 40
skill-sharing workshops
  benefits of, 154
  children's garden education
          programs, 158
  garden tool repair clinics, 157
  seasonal preserving workshops,
          156
  tips for, 155
slate, 85
slope, 31
snake plant (*Dracaena trifasciata*),
          117
snapdragon (*Antirrhinum majus*),
          98
softwood cuttings, 113
soil
  assessment, 26
  healthy soil, 26
  rescue plants and, 127
  seed starting and, 106
  soil parties, 150
  unhealthy soil, 26
space
  human movement assessment, 32
  human use assessment, 32
  insect assessment, 31
  light assessment, 27
  microclimate assessment, 31
  plant assessment, 29
  slope assessment, 31
  soil assessment, 26
  topography assessment, 31
  water assessment, 28
  wildlife assessment, 31
  wind assessment, 31
spider plant (*Chlorophytum
          comosum*), 116, 117
squash, seed collection from, 99
stem cuttings, 113
stepping stones, 83, 87, 91–93
sticks, 80
stone
  bluestone, 85
  crushed stone, 86
  outdoor furniture, 67
  stepping stones, 83, 87, 91–93

storage
  mapping, 28
  for seeds, 97, 98, 100
  tool lending program. 152
  for water, 28
Strathcona Community Gardens,
          145
strawberries, seed collection from,
          99
string of hearts (*Ceropegia woodii*),
          116
sunflower (*Helianthus annuus*), 98
sweet alyssum (*Lobularia
          maritima*), 136
sweet pea (*Lathyrus odoratus*), 98

T
threatened species, 122
tomatoes, seed fermentation from,
          99
tools. *See* equipment
topography assessment, 31
transplanting
  preparation, 123
  shrubs, 125
  timing, 123
  trees, 124–125
traveling suitcase program, 160–161
treated seeds, 103
trees, transplanting, 123–125
trellises
  architectural salvage, 76
  pressure-fit trellis, 80, 81

U
unhealthy soil, 26
universities, 49
Urbanite, 85

V
verbena (*Verbena bonariensis*), 98
vintage trailer guest house, 72–75

W
wandering Jew (*Tradescantia
          zebrina*), 116
water assessment, 28
water propagation
  native plants, 122
  house plants, 116
  tips, 111–112

weeds, 120, 127, 129
white Dutch clover (*Trifolium
          repens*), 136
wicker outdoor furniture, 67
wildflower meadow, 135–137
Wild Forest Zone (Zone 5), 39
wildlife, 31, 39, 53, 120
wildness, 16–17
wild thyme (*Thymus pulegioides*),
          136
wind assessment, 31
wonder, 21
wood
  branches, 80
  chromated-copper arsenate
          (CCA), 77
  heat-treated (HT) pallets, 78
  leaf composting, 82
  methyl bromide (MB), 78
  mulch, 82
  pallet wood, 78
  pressure-fit trellis, 81
  reclaimed wood, 77
  shou sugi ban woodburning
          technique, 79
  softwood cuttings, 113
  sticks, 80
  wood chips, 82
  wood rounds, 86
woodburning, 79
Woodland Zone (Zone 4), 39
wood outdoor furniture, 67
wood rounds, 86
World Trade Organization (WTO),
          100

Y
yellow daisy (*Chrysanthemum
          multicaule*), 136

Z
zinnia (*Zinnia elegans*), 98
Zone 0 (Home Zone), 36
Zone 1 (Garden Zone), 36
Zone 2 (Food Forest), 38
Zone 3 (Farm Zone), 38
Zone 4 (Woodland Zone), 39
Zone 5 (Wild Forest Zone), 39
ZZ plant (*Zamioculcas zamiifolia*),
          116, 117